Sir Donald
BRADMAN
A.C.

SIR DONALD
BRADMAN
A.C.

CO-ORDINATED BY MIKE COWARD

IRONBARK LEGENDS

IRONBARK
Pan Macmillan Australia

Royalties from the sale of this book go to the Bradman Foundation

First published 1998 in Ironbark by Pan Macmillan Australia Pty Limited
St Martins Tower, 31 Market Street, Sydney

Reprinted 1998

National Library of Australia
cataloguing-in-publication data:

Sir Don Bradman AC
ISBN 0 330 36082 5
1. Bradman, Donald, Sir, 1908-. 2. Cricket players - Australia -
Biography. (Series: Ironbark Legends).
796.358092

Designed by Mark Thacker, Big Cat Design
Printed in Australia by McPherson's Printing Group

CONTENTS

ACKNOWLEDGEMENTS

One of the challenges of this special and stimulating project was to find rare and previously unpublished images of Sir Donald Bradman. That there is a freshness to the photographic content of this book is a tribute to the thoughtfulness and resourcefulness of good and generous friends within the cricket community. To this end I have been particularly grateful for access to the private collections of Ronald Cardwell (photos p.20, 21, 25, 47, 49, 87); Tony White (p.53, 54); Ian Heads (p.13, 23, 32, 71, 73, 77, 78, 85); Berry Favell (p.91, 96, 100) and Sam Loxton (p.74, 75) and the paintings by Bill Leak (p.3, 117). I am also in the debt of SACA historian Bernard Whimpress (p.110, 111); Shyam Sundar Ghosh, the sports editor of *The Statesman*, Calcutta (p.63); S. Krishnan and Nirmal Shekar of *The Hindu*, Chennai (p.69); Michael Rayner/Sport. The Library (p.115); Bryan Charlton/*The Age* (p.109); The Australian Broadcasting Corporation Document Archives (p.79, 82, 112) and the *West Australian* newspaper (p.41). I would especially like to thank Sharon Doyle of *The Advertiser*, Adelaide (p.17, 28, 76, 81, 90, 94, 98, 102, 103, 104, 105, 107, 113, 114).

Appreciation is also due to Peter Allen of Allen and Kemsley publishing and Ken Jacobs, the affable and forever vigilant chief executive officer of the Victorian Cricket Association. The other photographs in the book are from the famed Bradman albums housed at the National Library of Australia in Canberra. Above all, I wish to earnestly thank Richard Mulvaney, the indefatigable director of the Bradman Museum, Bowral for his support, advice and encouragement.

Mike Coward
Sydney, May 1998

FOREWORD

by Richie Benaud

There has been more written about Bradman than any other cricketer, the boy from the country town who became a legend of the game and continues to be so, but this book is something new and the idea behind it is fresh. At 90 years of age and in the fiftieth anniversary of the 1948 Australian tour of England where he was captain, these pages offer a different perspective on Sir Donald.

Purely by chance, my own cricket career was linked with his, not as a fellow player, because he retired the year I started playing for New South Wales, but in a variety of other ways. In 1940, the first time I ever watched a cricket match at the Sydney Cricket Ground, he was playing as captain of South Australia; six years later, on the same ground, I saw my first Test match and he was captain of Australia. He was one of the selectors who chose me for my Test match debut, then my elevation to the Australian captaincy, and he was in charge when I stepped down from the captaincy and, later in the same summer, when I played for Australia for the last time.

I was a youngster in the Depression years in Australia, born in 1930 at the same time as Don was being flown across the continent after a triumphant 1930 tour of England, where he confirmed most of the predictions of what he would do to England's bowlers. And he was a legspinner. Like all legends there are stories about the quality of his bowling, some being of the opinion that he could have been a champion in that area of the game, others that it was wise of him to allow Bill O'Reilly and Clarrie Grimmett full rein and not give up his own day job.

This book, though, is not about cricket styles or runs or wickets or types of bowling. It is about the way in which people knew and observed Don over the years, and the manner in which they believe he influenced them and the country. In these days of a far more affluent society it isn't easy for people to convey the difficult times of the Depression and how a young cricketer could become a hero, how cricket grounds would start to fill when it was known he would be batting and how spectators would make for the toast-rack trams when he was dismissed.

I grew up just down the road from where he was born at Cootamundra. It was a matter of a short car trip from there to Jugiong, on the Murrumbidgee River, where my father was the schoolteacher. It was, though, a far longer and more difficult trip to the moment where he stood, as chairman of the Australian selectors, the night before the Tied Test in Brisbane in 1960, and delivered to the players a message which had a profound effect on cricket in Australia that summer and in the immediate future. He was able to do that because he had the most incisive and brilliant mind of any cricketer and administrator the cricket world has known.

Capturing those matters and placing them on record with care, attention, accuracy and, above all, with feeling, has been entrusted to the authors of this book and they have produced a splendid publication. More importantly, they have been able to underline for others that he is not just a cricketer, knighted for his services to the game, but a youngster born in a country area in difficult times who was able to become a national hero.

Don Bradman

EXPLORING FRONTIERS

by Rodney Cavalier

*Presently the Deputy Chairman of the
National Council for the Centenary of
Federation, Rodney Cavalier is a
Trustee of the Sydney Cricket Ground.
He has been a New South Wales
Minister for Education and a writer
on cricket.*

Page 5: Boy's best friend. A previously unseen photograph of Don Bradman, in Bowral school uniform, with the family terrier, Teddy, at home on the veranda at Shepherd Street, Bowral.

Opposite: Sartorial splendour. Bradman (right) and brother Vic dressed to kill and happy to pose for this photograph in the backyard of the Glebe Street, Bowral, home to which the family moved in 1924.

Right: Bradman with one of his mentors, Alf Stephens, a Bowral builder and town mayor, who closely followed Bradman's fortunes and more than once travelled to England to see him play.

n the final years before the First World War, George Bradman and Emily (née Whatman) settled in the town of Bowral, a little over 100 kilometres south of Sydney. They were bringing their five children to a prospering middle-class community with a population fewer than 2000.

The arrival of the railway in the 1860s had brought Bowral within easy distance of those of Sydney's well-to-do in search of a cooler climate, a sense of space and a variation in the seasons. Guesthouses and hotels catered for the visitor, subdivisions of the big holdings near to the town enabled the construction of substantial mansions, gatehouses and gardeners' cottages.

The new estates needed tradespeople and supplies. Locals who positioned their enterprises to meet those demands could accumulate considerable wealth within a generation. One such local was Alf Stephens, proprietor of a joinery shop, into whose employment entered George Bradman, carpenter. Stephens had inherited his business from a father of the same name. By dint of his own endeavours he had emerged as the most powerful man in Bowral. President of the Bowral Cricket Club, often its captain, long-time alderman and mayor, powerful in all matters commercial, Stephens was the force behind sport and conservative politics in the area for many decades to come.

Employment with Stephens was never more than earning a wage for George. It required steady application to the tasks at hand and occasional hard labour: employment meant the certainty of regular pay, a very different situation to the survival farming

The patriarch, his sons and pals on an outing to Fitzroy Falls near Bowral. George Bradman (centre) is flanked by (from left): Frank Cush, Alf Stephens, Ted Adams, Vic Bradman, Don Bradman, Hugh Fraser, Dick Jones and Mick Morgan.

which he and Emily had known for all of their married life in the Cootamundra district.

George was only 17 when he married in 1893, Emily four years older. The marriage was blessed with children soon enough, three daughters followed by a son, Victor, born in 1904. Don Bradman arrived four years after that. The move to Bowral was a return for Emily, a return to a district where her family had been residents since the beginnings of white settlement. Like so many people who married young and with few prospects, the Bradmans appear to have set about teaching all of their children the abiding importance of constructing lives where each could make a free choice about the course to follow – the very purpose of a good, sound general education.

As a result of Sir Donald Bradman's own writings and the efforts of more than a dozen biographers, we have the image of a child pursuing his destiny from the moment he hurled a golf ball against the base of the water tank in the backyard of Shepherd Street. It is a picture of loneliness and discipline, the beginnings of the hand–eye coordination which would astonish the cricketing world.

The image serves the fable of a country childhood distant from care and the troubles of Empire, a childhood of competitive games, fishing, cycling, meeting young Jessie Menzies, and conquering the bowling from all comers. The image premises, as other writers have put it, a 'Huck Finn heaven' in which 'the First World War largely passed Bowral by'. It is a beguiling portrait but not one which withstands a cursory knowledge of Australian social history.

For a start Don did not live far from his friends. No-one in Bowral lived very far from anyone else; his home was less than a kilometre from the centre of town, only a few hundred metres to Glebe Park where serious cricket was on offer. If Don spent a lot of time alone, it was because he chose to. Don was approaching six when the War broke out and 10 when it ended. Australian society had changed forever. Don did not escape its impact; he could not have been unaware of it.

By late 1914 the children of Bowral School were beginning their regular participation in the patriotic drives that characterised the home front. At St Jude's each Sunday for all of the four years of war his family sat through sermons and remembrance. In the months before Gallipoli, when the causes for involvement required tangible expression, Bowral had adopted benighted Belgium as its own. On 27 April 1915, before any news of the fateful landing two days earlier, the Bowral v Kangaloon-Mittagong game (George opened and scored 15) was an occasion when the crowd responded to an appeal to help the Belgians. Bowral was comfortably behind the war effort.

Belgian Day saw the local towns totally devoted to fundraising. All businesses closed for two hours. Schoolchildren led the patriotic

Right: Tomorrow belongs to me. Don Bradman, aged 17 and with a spring in his step and a glint in his eye, at the end of his first full season with the Bowral Town cricket team in 1925–26.

Opposite: Half a century after scoring the first century in Test cricket, Charles Bannerman met 19-year-old Don Bradman who was destined to score 29 Test hundreds. Bannerman died in August 1930 at the age of 79, two days before Australia regained the Ashes and Bradman completed his astonishing maiden tour of England.

chorus. By June the local newspaper noted that Bowral had raised £1139, a veritable fortune for the time.

With voluntary recruiting faltering at the end of 1915, a group of men from Wagga Wagga began a 'snowball march' – intended to gather recruits wherever it stopped. Its route passed through Bowral, a big occasion, met with big crowds, a recruiting rally – yet not a soul enlisted.

It was the first signal that Bowral had gone sour on the War. Rural dwellers questioned whether there was an end to the appetite of the War for their young men. The issue of conscription split Bowral: 1916 was beset with bitter debate. The national plebiscite occasioned weeks of nightly meetings for both sides of the issue in all the settlements of the district, including the largest crowd ever assembled at the Empire Cinema – larger than the population of Bowral itself, larger even than the send-off for the Don in 1930. No household escaped the implications. George was of conscriptable age, Victor was approaching. The male friends of the sisters and their friends were away at war or contemplating departure.

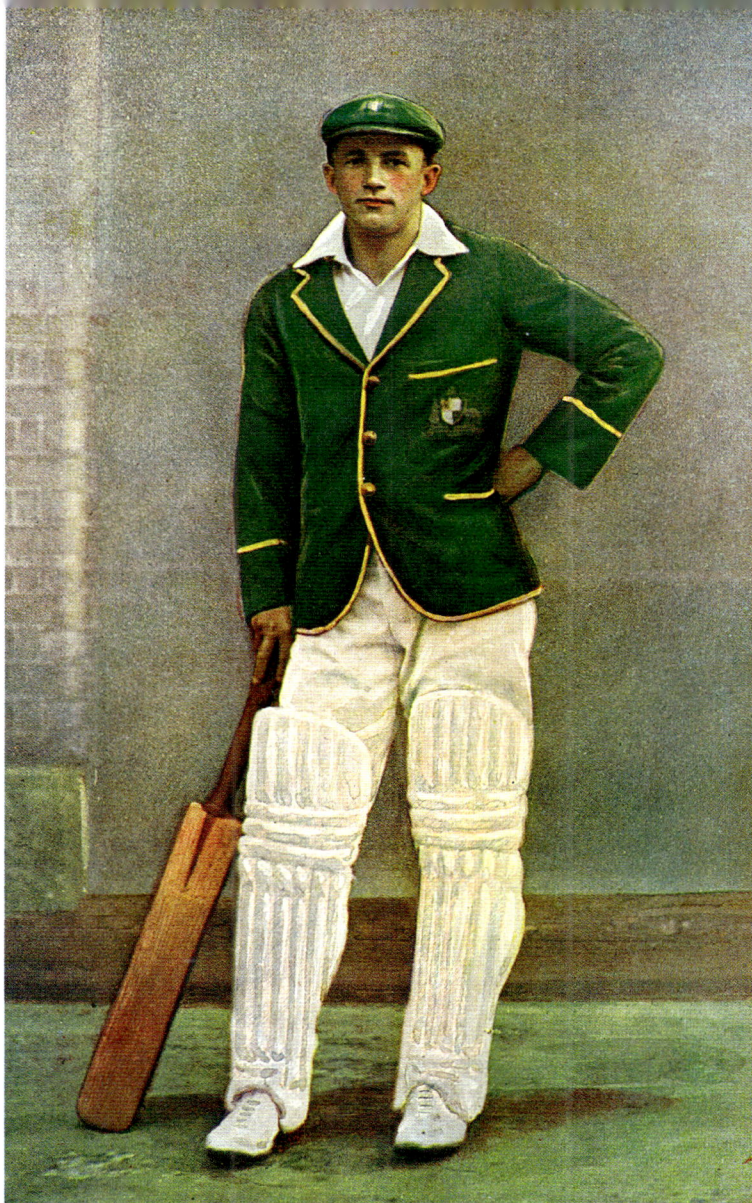

Opposite: **The future face of Australian and world cricket. An intimate study of Bradman during his first Test match at the Exhibition Ground, Brisbane, from 30 November 1928.**

Right: **One of the first full-page spreads devoted to the rising star of the sporting galaxy. This supplement to the** *Australian Sporting and Dramatic News*, **23 March 1929, referred to Bradman as Australia's record-breaking colt – a hero of the 1928–29 Test matches.**

In spite of a campaign which called into question the loyalty of those opposed to conscription, the residents of Bowral voted to reject compulsion by 488–477. People once friends stopped talking to each other. The story of Bowral's No vote is suppressed in all of its histories, concentrating as they do on men who went to war and the memorials in their honour. Only in Glenquarry, on the crest of the hill directly above the Menzies farm, is there a reminder of what those divisions meant. Glenquarry built a meeting hall after the War and called it a 'Peace Memorial'. Don had to pass that hall every time he visited Jessie.

The surnames of the players in the Bowral cricket team are consonant with the names of recruits and the war dead. Young men who played with George did not return, older men who played with George and Don had sons who did not return. In September 1916 Shepherd Street learned of the death of a resident, Private J.J.G. Riley. In the streets of Bowral for all the years between the Wars was the constant sight of men whose bodies had been wrecked by the war. The grieving of widows and fatherless children, Don's contemporaries, was a reality behind the need of Bowral, like Australia, to make sense of its grief and get on with living.

Cricket continued throughout, life had to go on. *The Southern Mail* carried notices from G. Bradman, Hon Secretary of the

Berrima District Cricket Association, setting out the organisational details of a competition based on the major towns of Bowral, Moss Vale and Mittagong and the tiny settlements which were always struggling to field a team. The matches played by Bowral were hard affairs; batsmen continued until dismissed – there was no such thing as retirement – declarations were made only when the innings total was nigh-unreachable.

In addition to his duties with the District, George was Assistant Secretary and Treasurer of the Bowral Club and a selector. The nature of George's world brought him home for most nights of his children's childhood, his work for cricket was a part of their home life. Perhaps there is another image of the young Bradman, one as beguiling as the golf ball against the water tank: an image of all the family at home, a father at the kitchen table under the flickering light of a kerosene lamp, working on the correspondence and the minutes of the local cricket clubs. The very young Don will not understand what his father is doing and then, one day, he will. In due course he will be absorbed by these silent labours and want to become a part of them.

Before he was old enough to be playing, he was appointed scorer for the Bowral Club, a position of significance in a club which took its cricket so seriously. The scorer was wholly absorbed in the progress of a match. Like the umpires, he could not relax for a single ball. Before Don famously substituted for a missing player, he was learning so much about the game by scrutinising the strengths and weaknesses of players and wickets and circumstance.

The celebrated visit to the Sydney Cricket Ground in the company of his father to see the first Test of the 1920–21 Ashes series takes its place in the Bradman legend as a life-changing moment for Don – as the first visit to the SCG remains for anyone who has ever loved sport. Yet, three months earlier, back in Bowral, Don had revealed a commitment to cricket well beyond the game on the field. Having seen how the game worked behind the scenes as Alf Stephens, his father and a small coterie kept the club and the district viable, Don wanted to see for himself what happened at night when the men assembled in committee to arrange the coming season. In September 1920 Don Bradman attended the annual general meeting of the Bowral Cricket Club. He had just turned 12. He found that committee politics were to his liking.

Don was to attend every subsequent annual meeting until his departure from the district. From his father at home, then in the presence of worldly men in the formality of a meeting, he learned about the precarious financial basis of local cricket, the crucial importance of sympathetic local government to provide facilities for cricket's benefit at the expense of others, the logistics of assembling a team and transporting them when required, the hard

14

Opposite: Clearly the great English batsman Jack Hobbs was quick to recognise the impact Bradman could have on the cricket world and wanted a personal photograph for posterity. Hobbs, who had just entered his forty-seventh year, asked 20-year-old Bradman to pose for this shot at Adelaide Oval during the fourth Test of the 1928–29 series. Bradman, batting at six in his third Test, scored 40 and 58.

Above: Seize the moment. Bradman makes a store appearance to extol the qualities of the Sykes bat which enabled him to score 452 not out for New South Wales against Queensland at the Sydney Cricket Ground in January 1930. Only two men have bettered this score – Brian Lara with an undefeated 501 for Warwickshire against Durham at Birmingham in 1994 and Hanif Mohammad who accumulated 499 for Karachi against Bahawalpur at Karachi in 1958–59.
Opposite: At the Sydney Cricket Ground nets, 1929.

decisions involved in streaming limited personnel into grades and separate elevens, the politics of selection. To the home team fell the responsibility of hosting the visitors at dinner, a duty faithfully observed by Bowral with all its attendant costs and organisation. While most of the players took no interest in the affairs of the club, this non-player could not get enough of it.

Before he was eligible to join, the enthusiast was made an honorary member. As soon as he was eligible, he was elected to the Social Committee; like his father he became the Assistant Secretary and Treasurer. The first resolution in his name defines eligibility for the bowling trophy to a player who has delivered a minimum of 20 overs. Don's attention to the organisation of the game was at least as painstaking as his mastery of batsmanship.

He had left school by then, his result in the Intermediate Certificate of 1923 was solid – 6 B passes, and A passes in Mathematics II and French. No-one has ever suffered from having to know the gerundive as a condition for playing in the First XI. A family or a school which does not insist upon performance in the full range of education and sports betrays the potential for genius whatever its expression. It was not a failure that George or Emily were ever going to make with any of their children.

Cricket was becoming a means to that end but no more than that. Don entered a local real estate firm whose principal was a part of Alf's network. Bowral was in the midst of a land and

Above: Bradman acknowledging the sustained cheering of the crowd after reaching his double century in his first appearance at Lord's during the last week of June 1930. It was to become a familiar scene.
Opposite: So buoyant after scoring 131 and 254 in his first two Tests in England, Bradman strides to the wicket at Headingley on the first day of the third Test, 11 July 1930. By the end of the day he had scored an undefeated 309 and eclipsed the world-record 287 R.E. (Tip) Foster made on debut in Sydney in 1903–04. Bradman was dismissed the following day for 334.

Below: On the Sunday of the fourth Ashes Test at Manchester in 1930, the Australian team were entertained by Sir Edwin and Lady Stockton at their beautiful country home, Jodrell Hall. Photo call at the end of a pleasant Sunday afternoon. Back row (from left): The Honourable S.M. Bruce, former Australian Prime Minister; Bill Kelly, Australian team manager; Colonel His Highness Shri Sir Ranjitsinhji Vibhaji, Maharajah Jam Sahib of Nawanagar, GBE, KCSI (Ranji), prince of cricketers; Bill Woodfull, Australian captain; Bill Ponsford; Bill Ferguson, Australian scorer; Archie Jackson; Alec Hurwood; Ted a'Beckett.
Front row: Clarrie Grimmett; Bert Oldfield; Don Bradman; Lady Stockton; Sir Edwin Stockton; Mrs Bruce; Charlie Walker; Tim Wall.

building boom, the wealthy from Sydney had rediscovered the delights of Bowral, a young man could discern a lot by driving them around and listening to their aspirations.

Learning real estate was his overwhelming priority: the Bradman discipline was such that he was able to put aside all games of cricket for a whole year and most of a second. He was getting the balance of his life right, he sensed the need to keep his interests in balance – he was not yet 17. His physical outlet was tennis yet he continued with his administrative interests in the cricket club.

He returned to the game in the summer of 1925–26 and within two years he was playing Test cricket. Bowral had afforded one final lesson in the politics of the sport. Don had made his Sydney grade debut but returned to play in the final of the Pickard Cup. Bowral crushed Moss Vale beyond trace. Don scored 320. The humiliation caused Moss Vale to appeal against the result based on the eligibility of D.G. Bradman to play for Bowral given he was no longer a resident of the district. The local association upheld the appeal, an outraged Bowral appealed to the authorities in Sydney, the matter was settled in Bowral's favour.

Some have sought to rewrite the Bradman story as a triumph against the odds, an unlikely journey from rural Australia to the lawns of Lord's and Sandringham. It is a view which blithely overlooks the organisation of Australian cricket; it was always throwing up cricketers from nowhere, uncoached and unworldly.

The Bradmans had picked the perfect town and the perfect time for a cricketer to grow up. Bowral was sufficient distance from

When not chatting with the distinguished guests at Jodrell Hall, which included former Australian Prime Minister Mr S.M. Bruce, playwright Ben Travers and the immortal cricketer Colonel His Highness Shri Sir Ranjitsinhji Vibhaji, Maharajah Jam Sahib of Nawanagar, GBE, KCSI (Ranji) the Australians turned their hand to a number of games. Left, Bradman shows his touch with a tennis racquet and, above, he follows his putt under the watchful gaze of team-mate Tim Wall.

21

Sydney to be a separate world, yet close enough for a traveller to reach it within hours. The town deified cricket, the cricket club backed their prodigy all the way. Don's emergence coincided with radio broadcasting and the newsreel, the basis of the mass audience for sport.

It is hard to perceive what element of the Don's magnificent triumph was against the odds – he had inherited uncommon prowess in all games; his parents afforded him the discipline and character to explore that prowess to the frontiers of the possible. Don grew up in a loving home, where cricket was encouraged but kept in perspective, a view reinforced by siblings who made no fuss about their youngest. In the entire history of Australian cricket it is not possible to find another instance where the odds were stacked more decisively in anyone's favour.

Above: Sales pitch. In the name of Sykes, Bradman and Maurice Leyland parade their trusty blades in a promotional exercise at Scarborough. Leyland, whose first name was registered as Morris but generally published as Maurice, was a distinguished England left-hander with an outstanding record against Australia – 1705 runs at 56.83 with seven centuries in 20 matches.

The emerging master, 1930.

REVOLUTIONARY PROWESS

By RONALD CONWAY

A consulting psychologist, Ronald Conway is a noted author and freelance journalist.

nternational cricket has lasted for 120 years, with the Victorian age its springtime and the early 20th century arguably its Indian summer. The 1930s marked more than the heyday of Donald Bradman as a batsman and cricketing legend. In Anglo–Australian relations these years virtually signalled the final days of the 'The Game of Empire' as Lord Harris often loved to call it.

As British rule spread around the globe, cricket had become a benign ally of imperial politics and culture. It bridged the old class lines of Empire by welcoming any sporting figure of talent. Yet, in the case of Australia, there were strong undertones of feeling that England merely patronised her colonial sons, while, for their part, the British resented the cheerful crudity of Australian spectators.

In 1878 my grandfather John Conway took the first white Australian team to England on a triumphant tour with himself as organiser, manager and twelfth man. He became the first Australian to challenge the pontiffs of English county cricket during a heated clash at Lord's with the great W.G. Grace as to which country 'owned' Billy Midwinter.

When Don Bradman walked onto the cricket grounds of

Page 25: A warm study of the maestro in the summer of 1931–32 when he averaged a staggering 201.50 in five home Tests with South Africa. In successive innings he scored 226, 112, 2, 167 and 299 not out. He did not bat in the last Test at Melbourne after twisting his ankle when his studs caught in the coir matting of the dressing-room.

Above: At home and abroad Bradman has received vast quantities of mail from admirers and well-wishers for 70 years. At the height of his career he received up to 600 letters a day. He has always prided himself on his capacity to answer as many letters as possible either by hand or with the aid of a trusty typewriter.

England for the 1930 Australian tour, he inherited the more or less cordial tensions of 52 years which had seen Anglo–Australian rivalry lift a traditionally sedate game. Bradman's revolutionary prowess at the wicket in the ensuing Tests undoubtedly shocked the ruling body, the Marylebone Cricket Club, into sanctioning the no-holds-barred tactics which led to the notorious Bodyline series of 1932–33.

A particular edge had been lent to cricket in the early 1930s by the onset of the Great Depression which plunged hundreds of thousands of the workers of Britain and Australia into deep poverty. In such desperate times popular sport was felt to be one of the few ways in which public spirit and private morale could be lifted. This was also the first significant period of radio broadcasting with the ABC launching its first Australia-wide broadcasts in 1932. Douglas Jardine's unpopular visiting team played to the largest attending and listening audiences since Australians had adopted the game.

For the third Test in Adelaide in January 1933, when public feelings about Bodyline were at their highest, the crowd was surprisingly big and enthusiastic. A great many spectators had travelled hundreds of miles by train from Melbourne and Perth. Relatively impoverished spectators were prepared to pay up to eight shillings for seats in the stand at all Test matches – a stiff entry charge for the time. While the 1930 Tests in England had shown

Below: Bradman presents a bunch of red roses to his mother, Emily. George Bradman, from Jindalee in the Cootamundra district west of Sydney, married Emily Whatman of Mittagong in 1893. Donald George was their fifth-born.

Bradman to be a prodigy, it was the Bodyline series and his efforts against one of the most ruthless of teams which made him a national hero.

One tends to think of the 1930s as a drab period overshadowed by economic crisis at one end and darkened by the threat of war at the other. Actually it was a time of technological and industrial innovation. The great arch of the Sydney Harbour Bridge was closed in 1932. South Australian rail links were upgraded and commercial air travel grew steadily up to 1940. In 1934 Queensland and Northern Territory Air Services combined with Imperial Airways to provide the first air-mail link to London via Singapore. In 1934 Victoria celebrated its centenary with the arrival of Henry, Duke of Gloucester to preside over festivities while New South Wales followed with the celebration of its sesqui-centenary in Sydney during 1938.

Partly because of her natural and rural resources Australia recovered more quickly from the Depression than either Britain or the USA, the worst period of unemployment having passed by about 1936. Australians now had more money to spend on recreation.

Radio and the talking pictures vied with sport as the great entertainments of the 1940s. In the latter years of the 1930s, chains of new Art Deco cinemas sprang up in almost every suburb and large town. Large movie houses became palaces for the poor as well as the affluent. Yet other building projects tended to languish because of scarce risk capital – our cities still showing much of the character of Victorian/Edwardian architecture left over from an earlier age. Food was usually ample enough but stodgy and light on vegetables. Even many athletes had never heard of

vitamins. Only the fully employed enjoyed a high-protein diet and

Opposite: Bradman was feted everywhere he
travelled after his extraordinary 1930 tour of
England. In this rare photograph, he is relaxed
in the company of Sam Jones, the mayor of the
town of Peterborough north of Adelaide.
Above: Pot of gold. Bradman with the
musicians who recorded his composition 'Every
Day is a Rainbow Day for Me' at Columbia's
Sydney studios in 1930.

Opposite: All aboard! Bradman peers from a train carriage during a tour of North Queensland by an Alan Kippax XI in 1931. The tour ended abruptly for Bradman when he broke his right ankle early in an exhibition match at Rockhampton.

Above: In lieu of a tempting professional contract from the Accrington Club in England, Bradman accepted a joint offer from Associated Newspapers Ltd, F.J. Palmer and Sons Ltd, men's outfitters and sports store operators, and radio station 2UE. This photograph shows him giving one of his radio talks at 2UE's Sydney studios.

seaside photographs of the period show a leaner, more sinewy male physique than today. Clothing was more formal, except on holidays, and most men wore hats.

Women in the 1930s were frequently employed in light factory work when their menfolk could not always get jobs. But they were paid significantly less for doing so. In the professions there were only a handful of women in law and medicine after World War I. But by 1933 there were 300 female doctors. Secondary education began to expand even though private schools provided most university entrants. It had only been a generation since even primary education had become compulsory for children in all states, and apprenticeships on very low wages were the only entrance to skilled blue-collar jobs.

Although Bradman was a household name during the period, other popular sports boasted their stars. Phar Lap probably represented the only occasion in our history when a horse became as famous as any person. Jack Crawford and Harry Hopman provided a formidable team of doubles players, Hubert Opperman passed into history as one of the world's greatest cyclists while nobody has ever matched Walter Lindrum, then in his heyday as

the wizard of the billiard cue. Australians even then were avid gamblers with the racecourse and the S.P. bookmaker as their chief outlet. No casinos or pokies for that generation, as the church watched over public morality.

Although cricket had barely been touched by commercialisation in the 1930s it had been inextricably involved in politics. As a noted Winchester cricket coach wryly commented of Jardine's captaincy, 'We shall win the Ashes but we may lose a Dominion.' Mindful that Australia had been made a completely independent nation by the Statute of Westminster in 1931 (adopted in Australia in 1942), there were countless ordinary citizens who felt that ties to the Mother Country had been as much damaged by cricketing quarrels as by bankers or financial interests in London. Certainly it took all the efforts of the MCC and the Australian Board of Control for International Cricket (now the Australian Cricket Board), to say nothing of many high-ranking political figures, to smooth over the ill-feelings of the white hot summer of 1932–33.

By 1936 Bradman became captain of Australia and his amazing career batting average of 99.94 was only equalled by his private peacemaking, elegance and chivalry on the field. The coming of World War II saw 'the game of Empire' pass and the 'game of the Commonwealth' take its place. The once rustic sport of gentleman players was never to be the same ... and neither was Australia itself. But Bradman endured.

Above: A part of his contract with the men's outfitters and sports store operators, F.J. Palmer and Sons Ltd in the early 1930s required Bradman to coach. Here the young and ambitious hang on his every word and watch his every movement as he demonstrates technique.

No holds barred. Bradman, whose key fitness regimen was running between wickets, executes a reverse headlock on amateur middleweight wrestling champion Jim Deakin.

FOR THE FUTURE READ THE PRESENT

By E.W. SWANTON

Indefatigable and influential Jim Swanton is a pillar of the English cricket establishment who has served the game with distinction as a writer and broadcaster for more than 70 years.

Page 35: Don and Jessie (née Menzies) Bradman on their honeymoon aboard the *Niagara* on their way to Canada and the USA with Arthur Mailey's composite Australian team, captained by Vic Richardson. The Bradmans were married at St Paul's Church, Burwood, Sydney, on 30 April 1932.

Opposite: Making their mark. Don and Jessie Bradman pose outside the exclusive Waterman's pen shop in Montreal in 1932.

Above: More attuned to radio speak since working for Sydney station 2UE, Bradman operates the heavy McMichael Super Range Portable 4 radio given to him at Fox Studios during his visit to Hollywood.

There is nothing in cricket history to compare with the initial impact of Don Bradman on the English scene in 1930. From late spring to early autumn, from Worcester in fruit-blossom time to Scarborough with its tang of the sea, on grounds great and small, he moved, apparently tireless, bringing into disrepair attack after attack in a succession of innings almost without fault. It was not an ideal summer, cool at the outset and more than averagely wet, yet only once did the conditions find him wanting.

When the Australian scorebook was closed for the last time it registered 2960 first-class runs for Don at an average of 98.66. There had been 10 hundreds, including one treble and five double hundreds. The only tourist from overseas ever to approach his aggregate (though at only half the average) was Victor Trumper who made 2570 runs in the wet summer of 1902. Equally unapproached are his 974 runs in a Test series, let alone his average in the five matches of 139.14.

Only 18 months older than Don I was lucky enough to be sent as a staff cricket and Rugby football writer of the *London Evening Standard* to a dozen of the Australians' 27 first-class matches, including all the most important ones except the first Test at Trent

Star gazing in Hollywood. Action, along with belief, is suspended to allow actors filming *Fu Man Chu* to pose with members of Mailey's composite Australian team on a goodwill visit to the USA. Boris Karloff is at the rear of the photograph with his arms around actor Ronald Colman and Australian captain Vic Richardson. Don Bradman is sitting three to the right of actress Myrna Loy and directly behind actor C. Aubrey Smith who toured Australia with England in 1887–88 and played his only Test match when South Africa entered the Test arena at St George's Park, Port Elizabeth, in March 1889.

Bridge. When the Australians first took the field at Worcester the three names following the captain Bill Woodfull's in the batting order were Archie Jackson, aged 20, Don Bradman, 21, and Stan McCabe, still only 19. We heard in advance that one of this youthful trio was a genius, and it was not Don but Jackson, already marked, had we but known it, by the finger of death. Having lost the last two series, Australia, bringing only four men who had previously toured England, had sent a young side with an eye to the future.

Within a week it was evident that in the case of Don for the future read the present. At Worcester, wearing one sweater if not two, shirt collar up, he scored his first 50 in England in an hour as if to keep warm, and then accelerated, so that his 236 came in four and a half hours. In the match following at Leicester better bowling curbed his style to the extent that he needed five and a quarter hours to reach 185 not out before rain settled the outcome. Don found that the ball turned and moved both off the pitch and in the air more than in Australia: the slower pitches suited his back play. Inside a week, with 421 runs to his name, he had adopted C.B. Fry's aphorism: play back or drive. His footwork when going down the pitch to the spinners was a model.

At Aigburth, against Lancashire, his great fellow countryman Ted McDonald, now 38-years-old but still as fast as anyone in the game, knocked out his middle stump for nine, and at Oxford on the Christ Church ground, Monty Garland-Wells had the effrontery to bowl him for 32 with a solitary shooter.

The innings he enjoyed most was the 252 not out which he made in four and three quarter hours at The Oval against Surrey

Left: Sporting giants. Bradman meets the immortal American baseballer Babe Ruth during a Yankees–White Sox game. Ruth is said to have confided to Bradman, 'Us little fellows can hit 'em harder than the big ones.'
Opposite: Power and anticipation. Bradman driving handsomely before rapt onlookers at the Perth nets in 1932 at the start of a white-hot summer.

whose captain, P.G.H. Fender, had informed his readers that Don was too unorthodox to succeed in England. 'It was a pity it rained,' said Don later, 'because Fender was just finding his length and I was getting my eye in.' On 31 May, thanks to Hampshire's captain Lionel Tennyson (grandson of the poet) staying on the field for an over in heavy rain, he reached 1000 runs by the month's end. No Australian had achieved this feat hitherto and only he was to repeat it, eight years later.

I cannot write at first hand of the 131 from which Australia might have saved or even won the first Test at Trent Bridge before Don, surely for the only time in his life, was bowled offering no stroke to a googly he failed to spot. The bowler was Walter Robins, that brilliant if mercurial cricketer who became Don's warmest English friend.

Of the second Test at Lord's I retain a clearer picture than of any I ever watched, partly because it was a great match and equally because it was the first of 300-odd about which I wrote or broadcast: 1601 runs were scored in the four days, the sun shone throughout and, well, Lord's is Lord's. There were heroics from both sides, Woodfull, Ponsford, Kippax, Grimmett, and Fairfax to the fore for the winners, Chapman, Duleep, Tate and Allen for England. But Don outshone them all with the chanceless 254 which he has always said was the best innings he ever played. It was the performance which established his pre-eminence without argument.

It was a match which, thanks to him, charted new waters. Four-day Tests were a novelty in English cricket. A side which made

425 in its first innings was not safe from defeat, that is if the opposition included D.G. Bradman.

I can see him now moving out to his first ball after the presentation of the teams to King George V had immediately brought England their first wicket: Ponsford c. Hammond b. White 81. He hit it on the full-pitch for a single to extra-cover, and so quick was he on his feet that Jack White was wont to declare that wherever he bowled Don could have hit him on the full. Tea intervening meant that there was 155 minutes' batting time left on that serene Saturday and when they came in at half past six, Don was 155 not out. He had given almost three hours start to his captain who was out just before the close – for exactly 155.

Australia having declared at 729 for six (the joke being that no figure seven could be found for the Tavern scoreboard), Percy Chapman made a brisk 121 in the second innings score of 375. Furthermore, he caught Don at short-extra with the best catch, Don said, ever to dismiss him and brilliantly again for one when Australia went in to make 72 to win on the last afternoon. It was, nevertheless, the end of an era, Chapman having previously won six Tests successively. As Don observed in his *Farewell to Cricket*, the result illustrated the axiom that fast scoring wins matches.

At Headingley a fortnight later Don was in even more copious spate as regards the ratio between runs and minutes. Australia having won the toss, there came the first hundred before lunch, another hundred in the afternoon and a mere 89 between tea and the close: 309 undefeated.

Next day, with the score reading 508-6, he was caught behind by George Duckworth for 334. Duckworth had missed the only chance Don gave at 273 when just 14 runs away from R.E. Foster's 287 at Sydney which had led the field since 1903–04. I had watched at Lord's from a press annexe at square leg, from which one could best appreciate both Don's faultless judgement of length and his speed of foot when he left his crease to the slow bowlers. At Headingley, from end-on, one could only marvel at the range and certainty of stroke which constantly beat the fielders on an unusually fast surface. To be exact his runs consisted of 46 fours, six threes, 26 twos, and 80 singles and his innings lasted six and a quarter hours. His double hundred in 214 minutes, 20 minutes ahead of Lord's, remains the fastest ever in Tests.

Following-on, England lost only three wickets in the last three hours of play, the first falling when Don brilliantly ran out Hobbs from deep mid-off. In his youth there was no finer middle or long distance fielder.

How on these easy-paced, plumb pitches to curb the phenomenon? Happily, for England, relief was at hand in the shape of a slow, turning Old Trafford pitch and high-class wristspin bowling from Ian Peebles, against whom Don was surprisingly uncomfortable. Nearly bowled first ball, he was missed at slip

Opposite: With his captain Bill Woodfull at his side, Bradman resumes after tea against Somerset in 1934. In poor health and poor form, Bradman was out for 17, another subduing result following scores of 29, 25, 36 and 13 in the first two Test matches.

Above: Unsurprisingly, there are few photographs showing Bradman carrying the drinks. He was only once officially 12th man – for the second Test with England at Sydney in December 1928. He was given the task after failing in his Test debut in Brisbane a fortnight earlier when he scored 18 (batting at number seven) and 1 (batting at six). This photo was taken at Sydney in the final Test of the infamous Bodyline series in February 1933 when a blow on the arm from Harold Larwood kept him off the ground for a time and he assisted with dressing-room duties.

Above: Paying reverence. Another crowd rises to the Don at The Oval in 1930.

before edging a leg-break to second slip for 14. Don admitted he could not spot the googly. 'We felt a new star had arisen,' he wrote.

At The Oval in the Ashes-decider, due to be played to a finish, Don accorded every respect to Peebles (who had the extraordinary figures of 6-204 from 71 overs in a total of 695). But he mastered everyone else to the tune of 232, and so had the major part in Australia's innings victory. Australia's vice-captain, Vic Richardson, summing up the tour, declared that Australia could have won the series without Bradman but they could not have done so without Grimmett. Richardson had a point in that Grimmett took 29 wickets and no-one else had more than 13.

It was, however, scarcely a generous estimation of the young man whose achievements had had no parallel, and have never had since.

Four years after failing to lure him to play in India, the Maharajkumar of Vizianagram, a small principality in Andhra Pradesh in southern India, sought the counsel of Bradman in England. Vizzy, as he was known, captained India and was an influential administrator who battled his highness the Maharajadhiraj of Patiala for control of Indian cricket in the early 1930s.

MY MATE GEORGE

By SAM LOXTON

*An incorrigible wit and raconteur,
Sam Loxton is a former Test cricketer
and national selector who for 24 years
was a prominent Liberal state
parliamentarian in Victoria.*

'It is, it seems, pleasant to be an Australian and to feel you have a stake in Don Bradman.' These were the carefully considered words of the late John Arlott, the distinguished and distinctive broadcaster and writer, during Bradman's farewell tour of England with his famous 'Invincibles' in 1948.

Remarkably, the words have a certain resonance 50 years later.

Arlott doubted whether Bradman found the situation quite so pleasant and confessed he did not know of a cricketer who would have changed places with him.

Nor do I.

The man I have known for more than 50 years, my friend variously known to me as Don, George or even 'Braddles', is neither shy nor reclusive as popular opinion might suggest.

But there is a natural reserve born of the fact that for 70 years his every word could have qualified for publication and therefore been open to interpretation and misinterpretation.

Consequently, while conversation might become an art form it can cease to be a pleasure.

Of course, Don's misgivings about the press are well known and documented. His greatest critics, Jack Fingleton and Bill O'Reilly who both played under his captaincy, let their bias, jealousy and animosity rise to the surface in their writings.

Again, it was Arlott who observed, 'Bradman ignored the spite of those who grudged him, kept his temper and consolidated a great public reputation. He gained more of respect than of envy from those who sought to understand.'

So very true.

Page 47: Bradman established his impressive reputation as a captain in his first series at the helm against England in 1936–37. After losing the first two Tests by substantial margins the Australians hit back with a vengeance to win the last three Tests with Bradman scoring 13, 270, 26, 212 and 169. Here Bradman and his counterpart and good friend, Gubby Allen, toss before the final Test at Melbourne which Australia won by an innings and 200 runs.

Opposite: History shows it was anything but plain sailing for Bradman in England in 1934. Soon after arriving for his second tour of the Old Dart he called on Mr Williams Sykes, the English cricket bat manufacturer whose bats brought him such success and fame throughout the vast Commonwealth. This rare photograph shows him with Mr and Mrs Sykes in the expansive gardens of their home.

Left: An incomparable combination. Two partnerships between Bradman and the redoubtable Bill Ponsford in 1934 continue to stand the test of time. No Australians have managed to surpass their 451 for the second wicket at The Oval, nor their 388 for the fourth wicket at Leeds, where this photograph was taken.

Right: With characteristic poise Bradman (244) pulls square during his world-record second-wicket stand of 451 with Bill Ponsford (266) in the Ashes-deciding fifth Test at The Oval, 1934. Their partnership stood as the benchmark until 1997 when Sanath Jayasuriya (340) and Roshan Mahanama (225) pooled their resources for a colossal 576, a world record for any wicket, for Sri Lanka against India at the Premadasa Stadium in Colombo.

Opposite: At the end of the 1934 tour Bradman fell gravely ill with an infected appendix and King George V was among those who monitored the maestro's condition by the hour and then the day. When Bradman's condition worsened because of peritonitis there were reports of his death. As the distinguished writer Neville Cardus was asked by his editor to prepare an obituary, Jessie Bradman left home for London at just a few hours' notice. Bradman said later he had 'hovered on the brink of eternity'. There was widespread rejoicing when he was officially described as 'convalescent' and permitted to leave hospital for a short car ride with John Lee (left), the Harley Street surgeon who first diagnosed his condition.

Don and I met for the first time at Adelaide Oval on 8 November 1947 during a Sheffield Shield match between Victoria and South Australia.

It was a sunny day – at least until I began to bowl. Suffice it to say my introduction to the attack led to our first conversation.

My first delivery to him had both pace and direction. Nevertheless, at greater pace it found its way to the boundary between square leg and fine leg.

While my 10 companions were contemplating just how long the over could take to bowl (they were of eight balls in those days) I exclaimed, 'Turn it up, that was a good ball.'

Wearing the broadest of smiles, Don's riposte was succinct: 'But a better shot, Sammy.'

These were his first words to me and we have been the best of mates ever since. Of course he went on to make a century, his ninety-ninth in first-class cricket, as it happened.

By some miracle, six days later I found myself playing under his captaincy in an Australian XI against the Indians at the Sydney Cricket Ground and it was a thrill to be so near him when he scored his hundredth first-class hundred.

When Don started playing Test cricket he quickly became the hero of every youngster in the country and I was no exception.

I was only seven when he played his first Test in 1928 and I

Below: Fortified. Some of Bradman's convalescence was spent with Jessie in Perth, Scotland, as the guests of the whisky magnate Mr A.K. Bell and his wife.

Opposite: Regal response. The Governor of Victoria, Lord Huntingfield (Capt. William Charles Arcedeckne Vanneck) KCMG, congratulates Bradman on scoring a triple century in his first away match in South Australian colours at the MCG in January 1936.

Opposite below: Chewing the fat. Bradman in earnest conversation with long-serving Victorian Cricket Association secretary Harry Brereton (centre) at the MCG, circa 1936. In deference, perhaps, a Melbourne Cricket Club commissionaire (far left) stands at his post.

never dared to dream I might one day meet him, play with him, serve as a selector alongside him and call him a dear friend.

How strange fate can be.

My Test career came to an end in 1951 but I continued at state level and, if anything, I saw more of Don when he attended matches as a selector.

There are those who believe that in his role as a selector Don was a dominant figure, given to getting his way and more conscious of state representation than other considerations.

This simply was not the case as my good friend and fellow selector Neil Harvey will attest.

Indeed, to illustrate the point I need only to recall the season of 1970–71 when there were many combinations of opening bowlers against England.

When we came together to select the team for the sixth Test match in Adelaide, Don began proceedings by saying, 'We are desperate for pace in the opening bowling department. Have you seen anyone in your travels around the country who you feel we should consider?'

Without hesitation, Neil said, 'There's a kid in Perth who is pretty sharp.'

When Don asked for his name, Neil and I answered in unison, 'Lillee.'

After some discussion, Don said, 'I haven't seen him but you seem to be serious about this lad. Put his name down.'

And the rest is history.

Unless you played under him, Don never proffered advice to a batsman unless he was asked.

And more often than not players were too afraid to ask a man with such a record and reputation and such a commanding presence.

Certainly this was the case with Neil when he was my 19-year-old room-mate on the 1948 tour of England.

Like any newcomer to England Neil initially struggled to adjust to the conditions and after five matches he implored me to ask Don for some advice.

'You tell your little mate that if he keeps the ball on the ground, he won't get caught,' was all Don offered.

Years later and with our playing days well behind us I was sitting at Adelaide Oval with Neil and Phil Ridings when Don stopped for a chat.

When he left, Neil turned to me and said, 'You know, Sam, he never told me a thing the whole time I played.'

This concerned me somewhat and I sought out Don and repeated Neil's comment.

'Can you think of anything I could have told him,' mused Don. 'I suppose there was one thing I could have told him', he continued. 'On many occasions when the ball was pitched short in

Left: Touched by greatness. Seven weeks shy of his 14th birthday, Lance Duldig, captain of the first South Australian schoolboys team, is presented to Bradman during the Sheffield Shield match between Victoria and South Australia at the MCG the first week of January 1936. Duldig matured into a fine right-handed batsman and on the day of his 19th birthday made his first-class debut against NSW alongside Clarrie Grimmett in his last first-class appearance.

Below: In just his third appearance for South Australia, Bradman scored his fifth triple century in first-class cricket – 357 in 421 minutes with 40 boundaries against Victoria at the MCG in January 1936. He went from 60 at lunch on the first day to 338 at lunch the following day. Bradman's score remains the highest compiled against Victoria. Here Bradman and opening batsman Ron Parker (right) resume after an adjournment.

line with the off-stump, Neil gave himself room and hit off the back foot like a rocket behind point, usually to the boundary. There were occasions when this shot got him out and I could have suggested he get behind the ball and push it forward of point for a single. But think of the joy I would have denied thousands of people had I done so.'

Neil was on cloud nine when I recounted the story.

Knowing that I had the great good fortune to play alongside Don, many people ask what the greatest cricketer is like as a bloke.

Don is a loyal friend to those who have had the good fortune to be close to him; a thoughtful man with a keen sense of humour and a most gracious host, especially when his wonderful wife Jessie was alive and constantly at his side.

Don was a genius, a cricketer appearing not just once in a lifetime but once in the life of a game and it has been the greatest privilege of my sporting career to be associated with him.

Spirited away. Don Bradman strikes a ghostly pose as the 1938
Australian tourists join the fun as passengers aboard the R.M.S.
Orontes celebrate the crossing of the Equator.

THE UNSEEN GOD

By Vasant Raiji

A chartered accountant in Mumbai, Vasant Raiji is a former Ranji Trophy player and a respected cricket historian and author.

ndians worship a multitude of gods. In Sir Donald Bradman they have their God of cricket. God is perfect. In the eyes of the Indians Bradman is the perfect batsman. God is unseen. Indians have not seen Bradman play. God's ways are inscrutable. Indians cannot comprehend why, in spite of numerous pressing invitations, Bradman never came to India. Whatever happens is God's will. So if Bradman avoided India, it was Bradman's will. Disappointment, but no ill-feeling or rancour.

'One of the sorrows of my life was that I was not able to bring Sir Donald Bradman to India before his days of Test cricket were over,' bemoaned the late Anthony de Mello, a former president of the Board of Control for Cricket in India (BCCI), in his treatise on Indian sport. Since Bradman did not visit South Africa, the West Indies or New Zealand as a player, Indians have no reason to feel that Bradman treated them differently.

Page 57: With England 7-887 and his bowlers crying for mercy, Bradman decided to bowl to the indefatigable English batsmen in the fifth Test at The Oval in 1938. He immediately turned his right ankle in a foothold at the Vauxhall end and was carried from the ground by 12th man Ted White (left) and Chuck Fleetwood-Smith. Subsequent x-rays revealed a fracture. Bill O'Reilly, who bowled 85 overs in England's innings of 7-903 declared, cheekily waves farewell to his skipper.

Like the South Africans and the West Indians, Indians too experienced the pleasure of playing against Bradman in his home country. The first ever tour of Australia by Indians (1947–48) received his full support. The Indian tour was not expected to result in a profit but Bradman felt that 'the interests of the game should not be subservient to finance'. He was of the view that while Test cricket between England and Australia would always thrive 'it cannot remain in isolation and will be materially strengthened if other countries can match their skill'. He considered it the duty of the two leading countries 'to assist the less matured cricketing countries to the highest level of play'.

Throughout the season of 1947–48 Bradman tried in various ways to assist the Indian players because he regarded it as 'part of our responsibility to encourage and improve their standard'. Indian players found Bradman to be extremely cordial and friendly and he was always welcome in the Indian dressing-room. A most wonderful spirit of camaraderie existed between the players of the two teams. 'I love to play against Bradman and that goes for all my players because he is a great sportsman and a thorough gentleman,' declared Lala Amarnath, the Indian captain, midway through the tour. In turn Bradman found Amarnath to be 'charming in every respect and a splendid ambassador'. Bradman regards the season with Amarnath as his opposition number as 'one of my most pleasant cricket years'.

Opposite: Bradman, captaining Australia in England for the first time, smiles broadly as one of his minions, 23-year-old Jack Badcock, films the team's arrival at Southampton.
Above: Pied Piper. Flanked by opening batsman and noted cricket and political journalist Jack Fingleton, Bradman is pursued by a horde of children in Regent Street, London. They were rarely seen close together in later years when Fingleton was a noted critic of Bradman.

The Indians were overwhelmed by Bradman and his men. Bradman scored 715 runs (four hundreds) in Tests at an average of 178.75. In all matches against the Indians his tally was 1081 runs (six hundreds) at an average of 135.12. In the third Test at Melbourne he got a hundred in each innings for the only time in his Test career. It was also during this tour that he scored his hundredth century in first-class cricket. A film was made of the highlights of the hundredth hundred and when it was shown in England the distinguished writer R.C. Robertson-Glasgow observed that 'at the historical statistical moment, when Bradman was about to go from 99 to 100, there was the Indian bowler (Gogumal Kishenchand) trying to deliver the ball with one hand and applaud with the other, a feat that is beyond the most enthusiastic practitioner'.

Professor D.B. Deodhar, the Grand Old Man of Indian Cricket who lived to the ripe old age of 101, covered the tour for an Indian newspaper and recorded the following impression of Bradman's batting during the series. 'Bradman when 50 could confuse our attack and after a century could rout it to the fun of the crowds. He could have easily established some more records against us if he had meant but as one critic put it "he threw away his wicket possibly to avoid the slaughter of the innocents".'

Reviewing the tour in his memoirs, Bradman pays handsome tribute to Vijay Hazare and Amarnath. He was impressed by the soundness of Hazare and the correctness of his stroke production.

Above: Bradman's greatness as a batsman has often obscured his reputation as an outstanding out fieldsman. Here, in 1938, he has 22-year-old Len Hutton at full stretch to avoid being run out in the fifth Test at The Oval. Hutton scored 364, England's 100th century against Australia, to break Bradman's world-record Test score of 334.

Opposite: Transferring his weight at the critical moment, Bradman is poised as he cuts powerfully against Worcestershire in 1938. Bradman scored a double century just as he had done in 1930 and 1934. The wicketkeeper is Syd Buller, who, following his retirement in 1947, enjoyed a distinguished career as an umpire.

60

Amarnath, according to him, was a brilliant player who often took unnecessary risks trusting his eyesight and natural ability. Bradman defends Vinoo Mankad when the latter's sportsmanship was questioned after he ran out Bill Brown while in the act of delivering the ball. For him Mankad's action did not violate either the rules or the spirit of the game as backing-up too far or too early gives the non-striker an unfair advantage. Besides, Mankad had warned Brown before running him out in this manner.

Within less than two months of his last match against the Indians, Bradman was on his way to England for the last time. A large gathering of his fans were waiting at the pier to greet him and his team when the *Strathaird* docked in Bombay for a few hours. Bradman was ill and wanted to rest in his cabin. But the crowd would not disperse without having a glimpse of their cricket God. In the end Bradman came on deck and waved to his admirers who waved back with great enthusiasm.

In June 1953 Bradman and Lady Bradman passed through Calcutta on their way to London. The Calcuttans were thrilled at the prospect of meeting them. They were received at the airport by BCCI officials and local cricketers in the presence of a crowd of

Sir Donald Bradman at Dum Dum airport on Wednesday. He is en route to the U.K.—Statesman.

BRADMAN RECALLS A MEMORABLE INNINGS

His Hundredth Century Was Against India

Opposite: Attention! Lieutenant Bradman preparing for a PT session at the Army's School of Physical and Recreational Training at Frankston, Victoria, in 1940. Others are (from left): Captain Beddome, Major W.J. Dickens, the commanding officer, Sir Frank Beaurepaire and Captain 'Slip' Carr. A physical training supervisor, Bradman suffered from severe muscle spasms and was invalided out of the Army in 1941.

Left: Garlanded in the traditional manner, Sir Donald Bradman treads Indian soil for the first time at Dum Dum airport, Calcutta on his way to cover the 1953 Ashes series for England's *Daily Mail* newspaper. More than 500 people swarmed on to the runway and besieged the plane. Bradman spoke to the press from a divan in a hut on the outskirts of the airport and thanked his Calcutta admirers for the warmth of their reception during his brief stop-over.

some hundreds of enthusiasts who had made their way to the airport to catch a glimpse of their hero. The admirers broke through the police cordon and the Bradmans had to be escorted in an army car.

It is universally known that Bradman yearns for privacy and more so in his retirement. Yet Indians will not leave him alone. He receives a large fan mail from all over India which, until recently, he answered faithfully. Every Indian visiting Adelaide looks forward to an audience with him and unless Bradman has a previous engagement, or is unwell, he obliges. Then there are requests to write forewords to books by Indian authors. Hazare must have been pleased beyond words when in the foreword to his book *Long Innings*, Bradman wrote, 'Hazare was one of the most graceful batsmen it was my pleasure to see and perhaps the best compliment I can pay to him is to say that his batting more closely resembled that of the great West Indian star, Sir Frank Worrell, than anyone I can remember.'

Rusi Modi, a sound and attractive batsman who missed the

Opposite: Bradman the bowler. An occasional legspinner, Bradman was photographed in his delivery stride at the Sydney Cricket Ground nets during the second Test with England in December 1946.
Above: King and country. From left, Bill Edrich, Denis Compton, Bradman, the Australian captain, and Norman Yardley, his England counterpart, at a Royal Empire Society reception, London, in 1948.

1947–48 tour to Australia due to ill-health, was an ardent admirer of Bradman. Though the two never met, they became intimate pen friends. Bradman wrote a long foreword to Modi's book *Some Indian Cricketers* in which he recalls one of Vijay Merchant's acts of kindness. 'I can speak of him with great affection because in 1934 when I was nigh unto death on a sick bed in London and my wife had to travel half way across the world to be at my side, Vijay, a complete stranger to me and to her, very generously and kindly looked after her whilst the boat was in port in India. Such a kindness portrayed the man and for that she and I remain eternally thankful,' wrote Bradman.

Bradman and the redoubtable K.S. Duleepsinhji were no strangers. Bradman had scored 254 for Australia against Duleep's 173 for England at Lord's in the 1930 Ashes series. Shortly after Duleep's premature death in 1959 Bradman readily agreed to contribute an essay to the Duleep Commemoration Volume. His moving tribute concluded, 'He (Duleep) was one of the greatest batsmen I ever saw and no finer gentleman or ambassador trod the turf. He had no enemy in this world. We are the richer for his brief but glorious tenure on earth.'

Duleep, too, had the same admiration for Bradman. When once asked how Bradman compared with his contemporary batsmen, Duleep replied, 'Bradman was a race horse, the others were cart horses in comparison.' Hyperbole, perhaps, for Duleep was no cart horse.

Above: The 1947–48 season was particularly memorable for Bradman. Not only did he score a startling 715 runs at 178.75 against India in his penultimate Test series but also scored his 100th first-class hundred – for an Australian XI against the tourists in Sydney. Bradman established an excellent rapport with the visitors and here is seen showing a photograph of his children John and Shirley to Indian team-manager Pankaj Gupta.

Opposite: The eyes and expressions of the young speak eloquently of a deity in their midst as Bradman went in to bat on the second day of the fourth Test at Leeds in 1938. He duly scored a hundred.

When the gifted and indomitable Sunil Gavaskar broke Bradman's record for the greatest number of Test centuries, some Indians asked if he could be ranked alongside the master. Gavaskar himself said that comparisons were inappropriate given Bradman scored 29 centuries in 52 Test matches compared with his 34 hundreds in 125 appearances.

During the Golden Jubilee of the Brabourne Stadium in 1987, the Cricket Club of India invited Bradman to honour the club by accepting honorary life membership. When Bradman conveyed his consent, a large poster announcing BRADMAN ACCEPTS was displayed on the noticeboard. Members received the news with great joy but a joy tinged with sorrow in the knowledge that Bradman had never played on their magnificent ground.

I crave the indulgence of the reader if I end this monograph on a personal note. When I was 10 years old Bradman entered my life through a page in the *Times of India* which carried his picture and the caption: 'Don Bradman the wonder batsman of Australia'. It was the time Bradman had broken the world record for the highest score in first-class cricket. Since then Bradman has been my hero and I have followed his career right to his retirement.

I remember the day after school nets when the bus conductor, seeing me carrying a cricket bat, addressed me as Bradman. I do not know how much interest he had in cricket but I do know from his remarks what Bradman meant to him. I venture to guess that Indians know more about Bradman than their compatriot Ranji.

On another occasion I was present when friends at school argued as to whether Mahatma Gandhi or Bradman was the greater man. The discussion ended inconclusively. Schoolboys may be pardoned if they admire sportsmen more than they admire saints, social reformers and politicians.

Once during the mid-1930s a group of Bombay schoolboys decided to start a cricket club. It was agreed the club should have an impressive name, preferably beginning with the letter 'M', so the abbreviation would sound like the MCC. But then one bright boy suggested the club be called the Don Bradman Cricket Club. The suggestion was accepted unanimously and to great acclamation.

As an author I have valued Bradman's opinion of my work. Though I have never met Bradman I have the feeling I know him well; a bond established through correspondence. His letters and autograph are my priceless possessions.

How does one explain India's obsession with Bradman? Partly it could be due to some of his personal traits which Indians so admire. He is a modest, self-made man who is appreciative of the achievements of others. And as a husband and father he has been loving and caring. But, above all, in his chosen field, he was peerless. As Sir Neville Cardus observed, 'Imagination boggles at the thought of the like of him again.'

Bradman is flanked by K.S. Duleepsinhji (left) and Indian captain Lala
Amarnath at a reception at the Adelaide Town Hall in the summer of
1947–48. Duleepsinhji, nephew of the incomparable Ranji, played four of
his 12 Tests for England against Australia in 1930. His cricket career
shortened by poor health, Duleepsinhji was a special ambassador for India
at the time of the tour and India's High Commissioner in Australia in the
early 1950s.

DESIRE TO EXCEL

By JOHN GOUGH

*Retired chairman of Pacific Dunlop,
John Gough is a company director
and president of the Trustees of the
National Gallery of Victoria.*

first met Don Bradman when he was assisting with a fundraiser for the war effort with another legendary figure, Walter Lindrum. I was 13 at the time and obtained their autographs with accompanying quotations in a coveted autograph book – there was no greater possession for a Melbourne boy from Heidelberg. I carried it around for years. But then 'Our Don Bradman' had become a familiar expression throughout the country when the great man was at the wicket. Indeed, the sentiment was even conveyed in a popular song. Expectations of him were always high and invariably he delivered.

Many years later our paths crossed in business. He was a successful stockbroker in Adelaide and I was a younger executive at Dunlop Australia. Sir Donald was also a director of the South Australian Rubber Company founded by the Lodge family. The company was going through a period of change, becoming controlled by Uniroyal US and finally was taken over by Bridgestone of Japan. This was all part of the extensive rationalisation of the Australian tyre industry in the 1970s and 1980s. As a director of an opposition company I found he was always competitive, enquiring and cautious.

Page 71: Bradman cuts a rugged and jovial figure in this portrait published in a 1948 England tour brochure under the name of the great batsman, the 'Governor General', Charlie Macartney.
Above: Hands of the master. Bradman chooses batting gloves at Slazengers at the start of the 1948 England tour.

Below: After an absence of 10 years and the anguish of World War II, the hearts, arms and doors of the English were opened to the 1948 Australians who were to become known as the Invincibles. Clearly the return of Don Bradman to the Worcester ground at the start of the tour provided the media with a significant photo opportunity. Bradman, who had scored 236, 206, and 258 on his three previous visits to Worcester, thrilled the crowd by scoring 107 and the Australians won by an innings and 17 runs. It was the first of their 25 victories (and nine draws) on an undefeated tour.

His link with Dunlop really began in his early cricket days when he first branded a product. This was in 1929 when William Sykes Ltd of Horbury in Yorkshire first made a Bradman bat. Don recalls spending one Sunday in 1930 in their factory autographing 4000 bats. Indeed, he still possesses the pen he used. The Sykes factory was later acquired by the Slazenger organisation and so began his link with Dunlop Slazenger which has continued for 69 years.

Dunlop Australia, with its sporting division, Slazenger, built a powerful position for sporting goods in Australia. In the post war amateur years the company employed many of Australia's greatest sportsmen and they were given time off for training and for international competition, where they excited their countrymen and the world with their performances.

Certainly tennis was well represented. Adrian Quist worked with the company all his life and Frank Sedgman, Rod Laver and Ken Rosewall also flew the flag. In golf the company had a pre-emptive position with the Dunlop and Slazenger clubs and the B51 and D65 balls: Peter Thompson used company equipment during his remarkable career.

These were a rare breed of outstanding athletes. They were fine people and became great ambassadors for Australia and were admired everywhere. Australia was a small country but well known internationally for the status of her sporting heroes.

Then there was Don Bradman.

Too often today words of praise are effusively heaped on champion sportsmen, but if there is a true legend, a possible genius at his art, surely it must be The Don. Suffice it to say it is

Right and opposite: At court. Three previously unpublished photographs taken by Sam Loxton, a member of the 1948 Invincibles and a close friend of Bradman, at Frogmore, the home of Queen Mary the Queen Mother, on Sunday 27 June 1948. Indeed, Loxton recalls that he was taken to task by Bradman, his captain, for flouting protocol by asking members of the royal family to 'Smile for the Dickybird'. Bradman is pictured, right, with Queen Mary, wearing her trademark toque and, opposite, with King George VI and, far opposite, with the Duke of Edinburgh. When Queen Mary also agreed to a 'team photograph', top right, in the front garden of Frogmore, in Home Park just south of Windsor Castle, Loxton hurriedly handed his camera to Her Majesty's Lady-in-waiting so he would be included.

From left: Bill Ferguson (scorer), Bill Brown, Ray Lindwall (obscured), Ian Johnson, Lindsay Hassett, Ron Saggers, Don Tallon, Don Bradman, Ernie Toshack, Queen Mary, the Queen Mother, Bill Johnston (obscured), Keith Johnson, team manager, Arthur Morris, Ron Hamence, Keith Miller, Colin McCool, Doug Ring, Neil Harvey, Sam Loxton and Sid Barnes (obscured).

doubtful any successor will equal his deeds.

What was his gift? He was blessed with an eye more accurate than others and a co-ordination between eye, feet and hands that enabled him to perform at a consistent level not seen before, or since, on a cricket ground.

Furthermore, he also had the gift of determination and a desire to excel and he exhibited these attributes from a very young age. All cricket fans are familiar with the way he honed his batting skills with a ball bouncing off a tankstand at his home in Bowral.

Don Bradman came from a humble background and had a modest education, but with his ability to apply himself and utilise his talents he became a speaker and leader only to be compared with the greatest in the land. And as an after-dinner speaker he was legendary.

In January 1947 I left Australia as an 18-year-old on a troop ship to study textiles at university in Leeds. Yorkshire was then a great industrial area, particularly for wool and steel.

Opposite: Behind enemy lines. Sir Donald listens intently as Vic Marks tells the story of 'Test' cricket at the Milag Prisoner of War camp near Bremen, Germany, in 1943. Marks, a merchant navy sailor and one of the first South Australians taken prisoner by the Germans in December 1940, recalled using bats and stumps fashioned from scrounged timber and balls made from the twine used to secure British Red Cross parcels. A competent cricketer in Adelaide suburban competition, Marks captained an Australian team to a 3–1 'Ashes series' victory and was presented with an elaborate carved wooden trophy to mark the occasion. The fifth and final match was abandoned because of a nearby air raid.

Right: Farewell. At The Oval on 18 August 1948, nine days before his 40th birthday, Bradman led the Australians from the pavilion for the last time in a Test match. And despite his disappointment at failing to score in his final innings – four runs would have taken his aggregate to 7000 and his average to 100 – Australia won by an innings and 149 runs. His faithful vice-captain, Lindsay Hassett, is behind him.

The United Kingdom was recovering from its ordeals of war, and clothes, food and petrol rationing were still severe. Infrastructure was badly worn, the troops were being demobilised and life was hard and colourless.

Cricket is a Yorkshireman's passion and every one of them is an authority on the game. The 'War of the Roses' against Lancashire is the annual tribal battle, but the ultimate moment comes when Australians play England at Headingley.

There was high excitement at the prospect of Don Bradman returning to Headingley in 1948 and when the great day came the famous ground was packed. I recall the people seated close to the roped boundary.

Recently, I heard the celebrated umpire Harold 'Dicky' Bird

recall how his father walked 30 miles to see the game and later exclaim, 'The great man did not let us down.'

What excitement to be present for the Don's last Test century and he received the most magnificent, stirring ovation.

The great leaders complement exceptional performance with qualities of integrity, intelligence and judgement. And judgement built on natural skills is what Don Bradman has possessed in abundance. For all this he remains a modest and shy man, but one able to meet the greatest challenges in sport. He was unconventional but totally authoritative when performing his art.

A few years ago Don Bradman videotaped a personal message for shareholders attending the centenary annual general meeting of Pacific Dunlop. I can still recall him saying that his cricket bat agreement with William Sykes was built on mutual trust and integrity. 'Without that no agreement is worth having,' he declared.

One of my joys in recent years has been my involvement with the establishment of the Bradman Museum at Bowral. Situated opposite the Bradman family home in Glebe Street the museum is a delight for cricket lovers from all over the world and a wonderful tribute to a great man.

Below: Bradman's praises were sung the length and breadth of England in 1948 during his farewell tour. In recognition of his astonishing achievement in scoring a century in each of his four Test appearances at Headingley – including 334 in 1930 and 304 in 1934 – Bradman was made a life member of the Yorkshire County Cricket Club.

Striking a chord. Renowned American
harmonica player Larry Adler at an
impromptu jam session with Sir Donald in
Adelaide in 1957.

VIBRANT AND VISIONARY

By BOB PARISH

*A retired businessman, Bob Parish had
an outstanding career as a cricket
administrator and served as chairman
of the Australian Cricket Board at the
time of the great schism in the 1970s.*

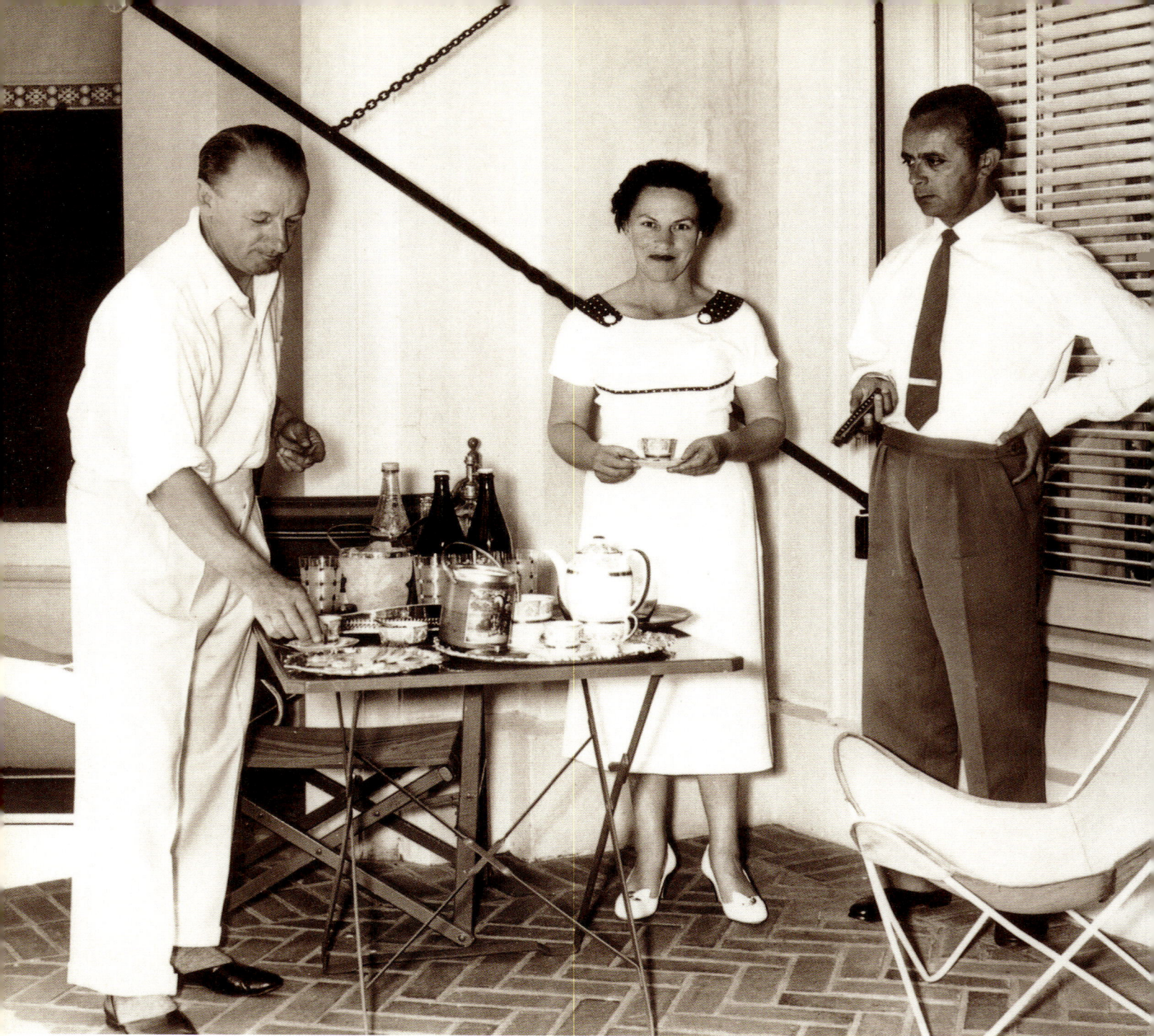

'Don't lose your sense of humour.' These were the words of advice given to me by Sir Donald in January 1965 when I was appointed manager of the second Australian team to tour the West Indies. Barely four months later, after the West Indies had defeated Australia in a series for the first time, I realised no better advice was ever given to a manager.

This is the series which is better remembered for the controversy surrounding the bowling action of Charlie Griffith than for the fact the Frank Worrell Trophy, named in honour of one of the game's greatest statesmen, was on offer for the first time. It was a challenging period in the lives of everyone on the tour.

A lot has been written about Bradman the cricketer, but very little about Bradman the administrator.

In part, this can be explained by the knowledge that Donald

Page 81: Homecoming. Jessie Bradman and children John and Shirley greet their father on his return from the triumphant 1948 tour of England.
Above: Tea and empathy. Sir Donald and Larry Adler break for tea on the patio under the watchful eye of ABC publicist Mignon Laurenti.

George Bradman was knighted for his services to cricket in the New Year's Honours List of 1949 – barely four months after his fortieth birthday and final appearance in a Test match and some years before he reached his zenith as an administrator and legislator.

But much like his career as a cricketer, his service in cricket's boardroom was extraordinary and unlikely to be surpassed. He had two periods as chairman of the Australian Cricket Board (ACB) from 1960–63 and 1969–72 and, for all but one year, was an Australian selector from 1936–37 until his retirement in 1971.

A man of great integrity, his greatness as an administrator lay principally in his vision and in his encyclopaedic knowledge of the game and its rich history. And, whatever his age, he always came to the table with the ideas and energy of the young and progressive. This is why he has remained a vibrant and relevant figure half a century after the end of his playing career.

In his earlier life as the game's most redoubtable batsman he had more than once been in conflict with the governing body.

Indeed, he had two celebrated clashes with the Board – the first for an alleged breach of contract after his magnificent maiden tour of England in 1930.

At the end of the tour he was called before the Board and £50 was withheld from his final tour payment because a book on his early life as a schoolboy in Bowral had been published in serial form in the London press up to the time the tour started.

Another disagreement followed two years later when the Board strictly enforced its rule that no player, unless his sole occupation was a journalist, could write for the press.

Bradman had never wanted to be a professional cricketer and had moved from the country to Sydney and accepted employment with a real estate company and then entered a three-year contract with a sports goods firm.

Towards the end of this contract he had the opportunity to go to England and play professionally with the Accrington Club but decided instead to accept a joint offer from Associated Newspapers Ltd, F.J. Palmer and Sons Ltd, men's outfitters and sports store operators, and radio station 2UE.

Bradman, however, was refused permission to play and write and, as a consequence, he advised the Board he would honour his contract with his employers and stand out of cricket. To overcome the impasse he was released by Associated Newspapers Ltd of his obligation to write.

Unsurprisingly, given it was designed primarily to curb his brilliance, Bradman foresaw both the dangers and ramifications of the infamous Bodyline series of 1932–33.

After the second Test in Melbourne – his first in the series – he told a friend, New South Wales Board member Frank Cush, that the Board needed to act immediately about fast leg theory. He said

Opposite: Under the watchful eye of his England counterpart Norman Yardley, Australian captain Don Bradman cuts a special cake to commemorate his last appearance in a Test match in England. Above: Standing on The Oval pavilion balcony, England captain Norman Yardley (wearing a dark blazer) calls for three cheers for Bradman and the Invincibles after they had retained the Ashes by a stunning 4–0 margin.

it was a disastrous practice which inevitably would get out of hand and he feared how it might end up.

Cush declared, 'Well I've got to admit from where I sit I don't see anything to take exception to.'

Bradman's riposte was cutting, 'Do you know why you don't take exception to it? Because you are in no bloody danger sitting in your padded seat in the pavilion, that's why!'

Bradman was not happy with the way the Board handled the Bodyline issue. He felt the Board should have sought a conference between the manager of the England team, Plum Warner, England captain Douglas Jardine, the chairman of the ACB, Dr Allen Robertson, and Australian captain Bill Woodfull rather than sending, as he puts it, 'awful' cables to the Marylebone Cricket Club (MCC) in London.

Probably the major issue which occurred during Bradman's periods of chairmanship was the cancellation of the 1971–72 South African tour of Australia.

At the time the Board was planning the visit Australia hosted a rugby match with South Africa and Bradman saw barbed wire around the Sydney Cricket Ground and holes dug in the outfield and piles of sand for use in dousing smoke bombs and flares. Two thousand police were in attendance, 200 of them on the ground and facing the crowd.

Reluctantly, Bradman recommended to the Board that it withdraw its invitation to the South Africans.

The Board substituted a Rest of the World XI which was chosen

by Bradman in conjunction with the national selectors of the day, Phil Ridings, Sam Loxton and Neil Harvey. The World XI was a success and Bradman commented that the innings of 254 by its captain Gary Sobers, in Melbourne in February 1972, was the best he had seen in Australia and bettered only by Stan McCabe's 232 at Nottingham in 1938.

Bradman was a member of the Board's Emergency Committee during the World Series Cricket upheaval from 1977 to 1979 and his wise counsel was of great assistance throughout such a troubled period.

When closely reading a draft of what is called the 'Peace Treaty' he made no comment about a reference to the use of coloured clothing.

Asked if he had any objection to coloured clothing he said, 'Why should I? The Pinks played the Blues in Sydney in 1892.'

While he has an intimate and vast knowledge of the history of the game he is equally renowned for his progressive thinking within the game. Speaking in 1991 about the popularity of the limited-over game he said, 'The society we live in wants instant gratification. It is a changed world. It's a changed society and I

Above: Auld lang syne. Bradman joins hands with newspaper executives H. Ainsworth (left) and A.G. Cousins, OBE at a memorable farewell luncheon to Bradman and the Invincibles at the Savoy Hotel in London in September 1948. Opposite: Ray Robinson, arguably Australia's most distinguished cricket writer, casts an expert eye over the wax figure of Don Bradman which was first exhibited at Madam Tussaud's gallery in London in 1948. Robinson, author of many fine cricket books including the definitive appraisal of Australia's cricket captains, On Top Down Under, died in Sydney two days before his seventy-seventh birthday in 1982.

think the one-day game reflects that change. It is what the spectators want. They want action – they want a result. If it hadn't happened in World Series Cricket the way it did it would have happened before long somehow or another.'

Bradman has not, however, always been successful as a legislator. He was, and still is, opposed to the 'front foot law'. He believes that the law makes it more difficult for umpires to properly adjudicate on appeals for leg before wicket and catches at the wicket. In his opinion the lateness of the call also means it is virtually impossible for the batsman to take advantage of the no-ball.

Nevertheless, when other countries showed a preference for the front foot law he was the first to accept the decision. Just as he was the first to support the use of electronic equipment to assist umpires. He argued that anything that helped umpires to arrive at the correct decision was good for the game.

Long renowned for his speech-making, his address at the 1977 Centenary Test dinner was a masterpiece. He traced the history of cricket from the beginning, and his knowledge, delivery and sense of humour enthralled everyone present. He began thus, 'We have in this room tonight the most prestigious gathering of cricketers in the world's history and I feel very proud to have been honoured with the task of speaking about 100 years of Test cricket between England and Australia.'

He concluded, 'We should be grateful that we have been privileged to participate, however briefly, in the kaleidoscopic scene culminating in tonight's historic dinner. None of us will be here to see the next, so let us be thankful and enjoy this momentous occasion.'

Like so many Australians over so many years I am thankful for the momentous career of Sir Donald Bradman and consider myself privileged to have enjoyed his company as a friend and colleague in service of the great game.

Bradman, the legend, 90 years young.

Valedictory. Bradman leading his team on to the Melbourne Cricket Ground for his testimonial match the first week of December 1948. Characteristically, he scored a century – his 117th and last – and the match ended in a tie. Total attendance at the match was 94,035 and aggregate gate takings £7,484. Along with donations from collection boxes placed at the gates and proceeds from other functions, Bradman received more than £10,000.

Above: Do as I say and do
as I do. The master struts
his stuff for attentive
pupils and observers at a
South Australian coaching
clinic in 1959.

Long-serving South Australian captain and daring opening batsman Les Favell receives the good oil from Sir Donald after being appointed to captain an Australian Second XI to New Zealand in 1966–67. Favell, an entertainer who had a profound impact on the cricket philosophy of the Chappell generation, scored 12,379 first-class runs with 27 centuries at 36.62 in a thrilling career spanning 202 matches from 1951 to 1970. He played 19 Test matches and scored a century against India at Chennai (formerly Madras) in 1959–60.

OF ADELAIDE
AND THE
CLOSE OF PLAY

by John Bannon

*A director of the Australian
Broadcasting Corporation, John
Bannon writes and studies Australian
history. He was Premier of South
Australia from 1982 to 1992. As a
Lord's Taverner, member of the South
Australian Cricket Association and a
Player life member of the Adelaide
Turf Cricket Association, cricket has
been an abiding interest.*

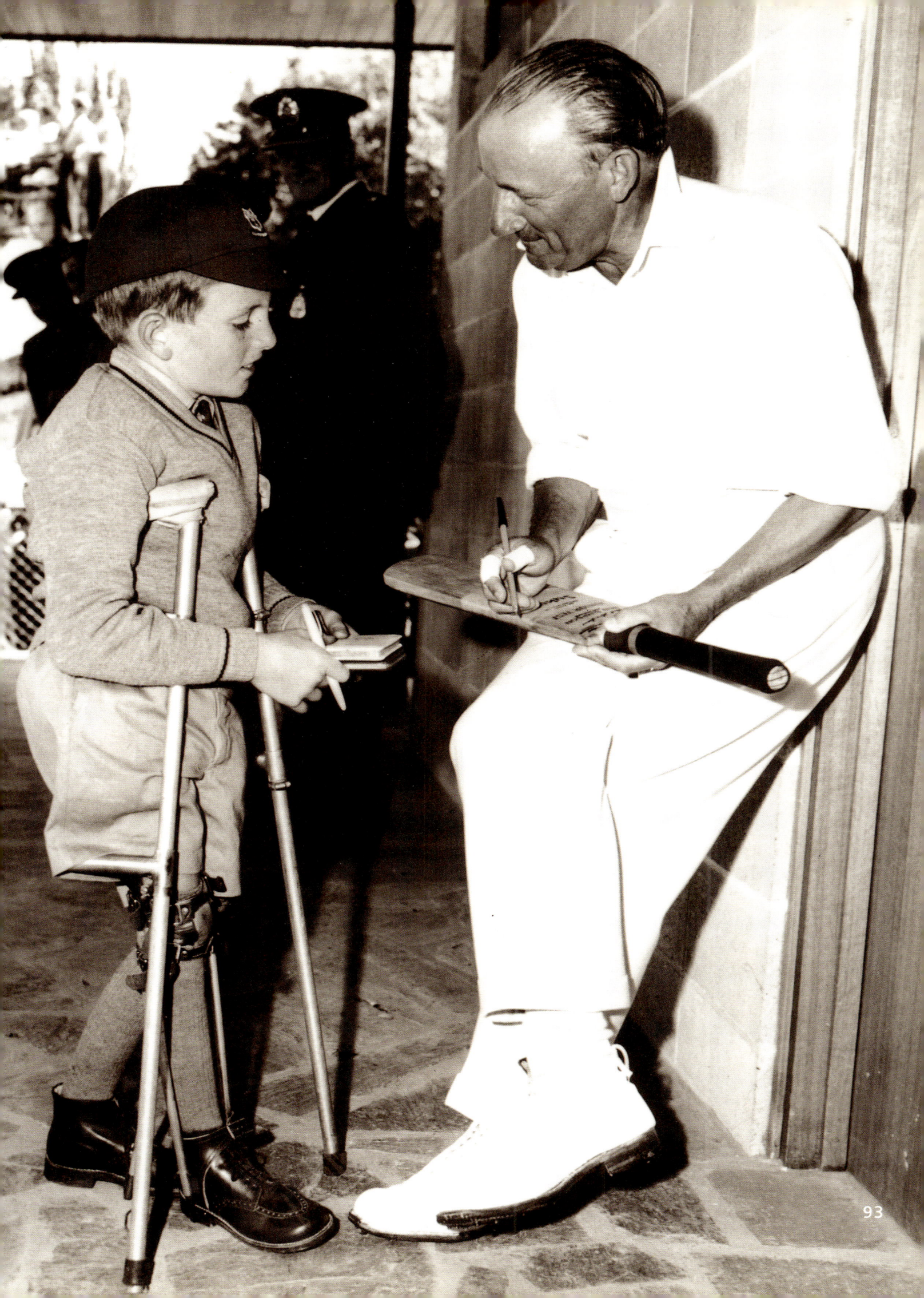

The cricketing feats of our Don Bradman are known by heart, but what of the fifty years since he retired from the field to his adopted city of Adelaide to lead the life of a 'private' citizen? Here are three snapshots of the later Bradman drawn from personal experience – the family man seen through the eyes of a child, the sporting statesman seen through the eyes of radical youth and the community leader seen from the world of politics.

A provincial city searches for identity and approval, symbols that confirm that it counts for something in the wider world. Adelaide of the mid 1930s was struggling out of a depression that had seemed to hit it harder and longer than most, when suddenly it had such a symbol. It was announced in February 1934 that Don Bradman would be leaving New South Wales and coming to live and play cricket in South Australia.

The enthusiasm and celebration that greeted the winning of the Grand Prix in 1984 was nothing compared to the euphoria of 1934 with the news that the ultimate sporting icon of the nation was choosing to make the central state his home. Of course the decision was not a simple one and wasn't really to do with cricket – although the prospect of working for someone who would not begrudge time off to play nor dock your pay for taking it was attractive. The key factor was the desire of the great cricketer to prepare for a career that did not depend on the game. Journalism, commentating and selling sportsgoods or real estate were not really alternatives to cricket.

Adelaide businessman Harry Hodgetts had promised to teach him the art of stockbroking and set him up for a business career. The size and location of Adelaide offered more chance of living a normal family life after cricket than in Sydney.

It was not an easy start – illness, family tragedy, the war, the bankruptcy and imprisonment of his employer, all made the first ten years very hard. A city of over 300 000 then and more than one million now, Adelaide nonetheless carries with it some of the atmosphere and attributes of a large country town. It was, and can still be, a hotbed of gossip and petty jealousy. Pride in the adopted son can always be tempered with some malice. There are still some who criticise or blame Don Bradman for those misfortunes.

It was after these years, following the amazing tour of the 1948 side and his retirement from cricket, that I first met him. We were fortunate to have as our next door neighbour St Peters College schoolmaster Tim Wall, whose family was great friends of the Bradmans.

Wall was Australia's leading fast bowler from 1929 to 1934. He toured England twice, played in a series against South Africa at home and in the Bodyline series, where he would have been quite capable of returning the fire of Larwood and company if Woodfull

Page 93: Eye on the prize. With bated breath 9-year-old Canberra Grammar student Ricky Scheeren waits for the signature of the great man during Prime Minister Robert Menzies' match with the touring MCC at Canberra in February 1963. Sir Donald came out of retirement for the match but, to the disappointment of a large crowd, received only five balls before playing on to Brian Statham. Opposite: Masterstroke. Sir Donald shares some thoughts on the relationship between the top and bottom hands with South Australian cricketers Neil Dansie (left) and Bob Lee during the summer of 1957–58. Dansie's distinguished career for South Australia spanned 1949–50 to 1966–67.

A galaxy of sporting stars in Adelaide circa 1961. Back row (left to right): Ken McGregor (tennis), Charles 'Chilla' Porter (high jump), Sid Patterson (cycling), John Devitt (swimming), Harry Hopman (tennis), Harry Gallagher (swimming), Sir Donald Bradman (cricket), Bill Roycroft (equestrian), Victor Richardson (cricket). Front row: Haydn Bunton (Australian football), Norma Thrower (athletics), Dawn Fraser (swimming), Shirley Strickland (athletics), Marjorie Jackson (athletics), Fos Williams (Australian football).

Opposite: Sir Donald and 'Nip' Pellew at a promotion for coaching clinics conducted by *The Advertiser* newspaper in Adelaide. Pellew scored two hundreds in 10 Tests for Australia and toured England with Warwick Armstrong's formidable 1921 team. He died in 1981 at the age of 87.

had not kept him on a leash in the interests of fair play.

Bradman had first come across him in the Sheffield Shield competition in the 1928–29 season, when he got his wicket twice in the match at Adelaide, for 5 and 2 respectively. That total of 7 remained Bradman's lowest for two innings of a match until, suffering poor health, he scored 0 and 6 for South Australia against Victoria in 1940–41. Wall was to bowl him for a duck in Sydney in the 1930–31 season. Bradman's wicket was claimed by 164 bowlers in his first-class career, but Wall was one of only eight to get him out five times or more. He was one of ten to get him out twice in the same match, one of fifteen to get him without scoring, and one of seven who did it by bowling him out. Of the 63 players who managed to dismiss the Don 'bowled' 78 times in his 338 first-class innings, Wall is one of eleven who did it twice.

So when Bradman transferred to South Australia he carried a healthy respect for a man who had become his friend and who was among those to greet him and his wife when they arrived. Nineteen years later, Tim's wife Ev accompanied the Bradmans to England as Don's personal assistant when he was reporting the series.

To a small, cricket-mad boy, Mr Wall's living room was an amazing place. There were not only memorabilia of Test tours and artefacts, such as the ball he used to take all 10 New South Wales wickets (including Bradman's) for 36 in one innings in 1933, or books on topics such as *The Fight for the Ashes* which I was allowed to borrow, but the occasional presence of the great batsman himself. I remember Sir Donald as somewhat withdrawn and preoccupied, not inclined to engage in small talk to small boys, although friendly enough. We hung around trying to remain unnoticed to hear the adult conversation, which disappointingly was usually not about past cricket triumphs, but golf. I was too young to have seen him bat but didn't need to – it was all in the head and in family folklore, particularly from a grandmother who had regularly travelled to the MCG from Bendigo for four decades to watch Test cricket.

The three Wall girls were great friends of the Bradman children and although they were older than us we often played together, with Shirley gamely involved in every escapade despite her battle with cerebral palsy. In the early fifties a cloud from time to time hung over the schools. St Peter's was twice closed and the boarders sent home when a poliomyelitis epidemic broke out.

Polio was ominous and serious, striking at random and leaving crippling effects, sometimes causing death. Before Salk and Sabin there seemed to be no cure, and the treatment was onerous, involving braces, massage and immobility. I can still picture the popular Johnny Gebhardt on his roller skates charging down the prep school path full of life and energy – then he was no longer there and in early 1952 we were told he had died. And then we

Vintage days. Sir Donald and fellow cricket knight Sir Garfield Sobers relax with Les Favell (left) and former Australian captain Bill Lawry at Gramps winery in South Australia's renowned Barossa Valley. Sobers, who played under Favell for South Australia in the 1960s, scored 254 for a World XI against Australia at Melbourne in January 1972 – an innings described by Bradman as second only to Stan McCabe's 232 at Trent Bridge, Nottingham, in 1938 as the finest he has witnessed.

heard that the polio had got John Bradman. Fortunately he recovered after painful treatment, with no great after effects.

John, like his father, tried to lead a normal life without attracting unwelcome media and public attention. His sporting prowess was considerable, a champion sprinter and hurdler who held state records, and a fine cricketer with bat and ball who, in his last year at school, scored a century and took a swag of wickets to help defeat a Prince Alfred College team that included the young Ian Chappell. But success even in his chosen field of athletics was overshadowed, and ultimately stifled, by extravagant hype as the media constantly tried to make him a clone of his father. Finally he made his own way as a successful academic lawyer with a new name and his family's blessing.

The year 1971 saw Bradman as the statesman of sport. The South Africans had emerged as a champion side against a background of the hardening of the apartheid regime and blatant discrimination evidenced by the d'Oliveira case. For their Australian tour of 1963–64 those of us opposed to apartheid had been content to hand out leaflets of protest before settling down to watch the game. Over the next few years positions became more extreme. The Vietnam War had swelled the ranks of protesters and raised awareness of international issues such as apartheid and racism.

By the time of the South African Rugby tour of 1970 it seemed

Above: Calm before the storm. Opening batsman Talat Ali in earnest conversation with Sir Donald before Pakistan's first Test with Australia at Adelaide in December 1972. Talat's right thumb was fractured by a ball from Dennis Lillee on the first morning but he showed considerable grit to bat one-handed at number 11 in the second innings to ensure the match went into the final day.

Above: Meeting the maestro. Sir Donald shares a joke with two of the West Indies' most redoubtable batsmen, Jamaican Lawrence Rowe (left) and Guyanese Alvin Kallicharan in 1975. In the background, Kallicharan's compatriot, batsman Leonard Baichan, gives his autograph to a young enthusiast.

to many of us that it was no longer a question of keeping South African politics out of South African sport. Sport was being used as a political weapon by both sides, and the tour caused chaos. Even in Adelaide, where rugby was a minor sport, a huge demonstration sought to disrupt the game, including arrests on the field during play.

For the Cricket Board and its Chairman, Sir Donald, a decision about the proposed 1971–72 cricket tour became critical. While public opinion polls showed a majority favoured the tour, a significant minority was preparing to protest, and the weight of international opinion and other Commonwealth countries including the UK were against it.

This was Bradman's finest hour – he canvassed opinion on all sides and reluctantly concluded that far more harm would come to cricket and the country if the tour went ahead than if it didn't. That decision, carrying the personal authority of Sir Donald Bradman, saved huge anguish and disruption in the country, was a significant factor in the strong opposition shown to apartheid by the South African Board and helped to rally opinion against the system and hasten its end.

Sir Donald did not leave it at that but earned even more credit by organising the highly successful substitute tour of the Rest of the World under Garfield Sobers, which produced a 'rainbow' side (including, appropriately, three South Africans) and some riveting

103

cricket. As a response to the exclusions of apartheid it was a multiracial masterstroke, and it was typical of Bradman that having made his difficult decision he then made sure it worked and was demonstrably acceptable.

A decade later, now well in his seventies, Sir Donald was still a familiar figure moving quickly through the streets in his three piece suit, hat low on his forehead, almost willing a lack of recognition by his demeanour. By the time you realised it was him, he was gone. But the successful businessman was gradually relinquishing the reins of his many corporate activities. Again it was typical that he left without fanfare and at a time when his considerable powers were undiminished.

During this period, while avoiding public events and

Above: Hero worship. Australian fast bowler Rodney Hogg seizes the moment to gain the coveted signature of Sir Donald. Hogg was feted as a Sports Star of 1979 after taking 41 wickets at 12.85 in six Tests against England in 1978–79 when the game was divided and emotions ran high.

Below: The way we were. Sir Donald and Clarrie Grimmett, the masterful legspinner renowned for his infinite variations, ponder their youthful pose as seen by a sculptor. The plaster sculptures, which were rediscovered in Adelaide in 1977, were first used on the Farmers Union stand at the Royal Adelaide Show in the mid-1930s when Bradman and Grimmett were at the peak of their powers. Originally the models were made to look as though they had been fashioned from butter.

interviews, he would attend dinners at Government House and was regularly seen at boardroom lunch tables. Banks, insurance companies and manufacturers in Adelaide knew that his presence would attract Cabinet ministers and other VIPs and guarantee a successful private gathering.

His knowledge of business matters and national affairs was considerable, but inevitably talk would turn to cricket. Without showing weariness or resentment he was always willing to gratify the gathering of suited groupies hanging on his words. Often someone would try to pit his memory of events or statistics against the Don, usually claiming first-hand memory: 'I was there when...' A number of times I heard him politely but firmly correct such tales and a check in the record book later always proved him right.

He was so well equipped as a speaker, host, and raconteur that with Jessie at his side he would have carried all before him if he had chosen to play a part in public affairs. He could have been the ultimate promoter of his state or, as a High Commissioner in Commonwealth countries, of the nation.

He would also have been a great political catch, although for some Laborites he may have seemed too conservative, and for some Liberals too undiplomatic and blunt – but his politics

remained his own. He resisted both sides while remaining courteous and open to both. He would have been a great Lord Mayor of Adelaide, with a profile and clout unequalled. From time to time he was seriously considered as a Governor of the state and may even have been sounded out for the post – but he had not come to Adelaide to lead its public life, rather he had come to find some privacy. For cricket he was prepared to step into the spotlight from time to time – but not for anything else.

More than sixty years on Sir Donald still lives in Adelaide, sadly now without Jessie, but having brought up his family, pursued his successful business career and established himself as a pre-eminent private citizen of his adopted state. The state understands that his choice of continued residence has always been a sufficiently eloquent endorsement.

If the hat fits ... Sir Donald hammed it up for the photographer at a meeting of the Australian Cricket Board in Adelaide in 1979. Enjoying the moment are other influential administrators of the day (from left) Phil Ridings, the late Ray Steele, Bob Parish and the late Tim Caldwell.

PRIVILEGES IN THE SHADOW

By STEVE WAUGH

Vice-captain of the Australian Test team and skipper of the one-day team, Steve Waugh is universally regarded as one of the world's foremost batsmen. A successful diarist and a collector of cricketana, he is well known for his interest in all aspects of cricket.

Page 109: The Master and The Man. A rare photograph of Sir Donald with Isaac Vivian Alexander Richards, the Antiguan, a man and cricketer of extraordinary strength and charisma who so boldly used the West Indies captaincy as a platform to speak out against racism, bigotry and elitism.

Above: Lap of honour. Sir Donald (right) with his longtime friend and faithful correspondent Sir George 'Gubby' Allen during the celebrations to mark 100 years of Test cricket at Adelaide Oval in December 1984. Allen, who was born in Sydney, was a fine all-rounder who captained England against Australia, India and the West Indies. An influential administrator known for his commitment to the game's traditional values, he was president of the Marylebone Cricket Club in 1963–64. He died in 1989 at the age of 87.

Opposite: Generalship. Sir Donald welcomes the incomparable and much loved Indian spinner Bishen Bedi to Adelaide. Every living Test captain who had skippered at Adelaide Oval was invited to return to the glorious ground to celebrate its centenary of Test cricket in December 1984. Bedi, a guileful and artistic orthodox left-arm slow bowler who took 266 wickets at 28.71 in 67 Tests, was at the helm in

1977–78. **He was joined by compatriots Lala Amarnath (1947–48) and Chandra Borde (1967–68). Sunil Gavaskar (1980–81) was unable to attend as he was leading India in a home series with England.**

Quite often a group of cricketers will get together and discuss their standing in the game. Invariably, comparisons will be based on statistics and all arguments will be settled by using the players' universally accepted method: 'Well, what did he average?'

Generally a player, or a select band of players, will be deemed the best of an era or generation. But none of these players, of course, can compare with the great Sir Donald Bradman.

However, some solace can be found for mere mortals in that phrase which often accompanies discussion of the batting genius from Bowral: Yes, but he doesn't count.

Sir Donald is in a class of his own. He always has been and always will be.

It is virtually impossible to put his average of 99.94 into some sort of perspective.

Today's Test cricketers have their own rating system. A batsman with an average of 35–40 is thought of as a good player. An average of 45–50 is considered the domain of excellent players, while anyone who betters 50 is generally thought of by his peers as a great cricketer.

But for someone to average just shy of 100, even terms of 'freak', 'marvel' and 'genius' and the like don't seem adequate.

For me, the very mention of the name Bradman conjures up many powerful images.

Initially, I see this little Aussie battler taking on and conquering each and every challenge that came his way.

I also see a man with a unique presence and an aura that shadowed him and engulfed everyone, especially when he was at the crease.

And I replay in my mind the priceless archival footage which, thankfully, has survived. And still it mesmerises me; those majestic, flowing cover drives and savage pull shots through mid-wicket.

In some ways I feel cheated there is such limited footage of the Don in full flow. On the other hand, this enhances the legend. So many of his deeds are left to your imagination and so his mystique and greatness continue to grow.

Perhaps it is meant to be, just as cricket was never meant to be conquered to the point of someone averaging 100.

But Sir Donald's legacy is much more than endless records and untouchable averages.

He is the symbol of Australian cricket; the heartbeat; the inspiration; the image of all that is good in sport and life in general.

Furthermore, his achievements show just what is achievable if

Above: Sir Donald pays his final respects to friend Les Favell, the dashing and influential South Australian and Australian cricketer who died at the age of 57 in 1987.

you are dedicated and committed to a cause.

Speaking with former Australian players such as Bill Brown, I am always spellbound by the tales of cricket's golden era.

This was the time when the Don captivated the attention of a nation every time he pulled on his baggy green cap and strode to the middle.

From what I can ascertain Sir Donald was ahead of his time. He possessed a hunger for runs that could not be sated; rarely hit a ball in the air; ran between wickets with great intensity; boasted a formidable fitness level; was quick on his feet; had the eye of an eagle; a strong mind and a steely determination.

In other words: The ultimate batting machine.

I will always treasure the experience of wearing the baggy green cap. It is a privilege shared by only 379 players (at August 1998) who have lived out their childhood dreams over the past 121 years.

To be able to follow in the footsteps of the 'Demon' Spofforth and Bill O'Reilly and other cricketers of such pedigree makes the cap so very special because it is the symbol that unites all Australian Test players.

But the baggy green assumes even greater importance in the knowledge that Sir Donald destroyed opposing teams and rewrote all the record books while wearing it.

For me, it inspires confidence, pride, commitment, courage and loyalty.

More importantly, it gives me an inner strength that I find comforting in times of uncertainty and self-doubt and for that I am indebted to Sir Donald Bradman.

Over the years I have played with and against many great players, but if I was to be granted one wish I would choose to see the Don in action.

In my favourite dream I have a vantage point high on the Hill at a packed Sydney Cricket Ground and I am watching Don Bradman, one of the world's greatest ever sportsmen, carve into an English attack.

It is a mild summer's day and the operators in the old scoreboard are working overtime as Bradman cruises to another dazzling century and hundreds of Stetsons are thrown in the air in tribute to the maestro.

This is as good as it gets; can ever get.

Above: Getting to know you. Sir Donald and genial West Indies captain, Antiguan Richie Richardson in a memorable promotional photograph for Slazenger.

Sir Donald and his beloved wife Lady Jessie in the backyard of the family home at Kensington Park, Adelaide, in January 1994. The couple moved into the house in 1935.

Renowned artist and caricaturist Bill Leak was commissioned by the Bradman Museum, Bowral, to paint a portrait of Sir Donald as he was in 1989 at the age of 81. In preparation for the work, which was hung in the prestigious Archibald Prize of that year and won widespread public acclaim, Leak painted two revealing studies (shown on page 3 and above) of arguably Australia's most famous citizen at the close of the 20th century.

STATISTICS

BRADMAN, Donald George

Test Career

Debut: 1928–29 Australia v England, Brisbane

Season	Opponent	Venue	M	Inn	NO	Runs	HS	0s	50	100	Avrge	Ct
1928–29	England	Australia	4	8	1	468	123	-	2	2	66.86	2
1930	England	England	5	7	-	974	334	-	-	4	139.14	2
1930–31	West Indies	Australia	5	6	-	447	223	1	-	2	74.50	4
1931–32	South Africa	Australia	5	5	1	806	299*	-	-	4	201.50	2
1932–33	England	Australia	4	8	1	396	103*	1	3	1	56.57	3
1934	England	England	5	8	-	758	304	-	1	2	94.75	1
1936–37	England	Australia	5	9	-	810	270	2	1	3	90.00	7
1938	England	England	4	6	2	434	144*	-	1	3	108.50	-
1946–47	England	Australia	5	8	1	680	234	1	3	2	97.14	3
1947–48	India	Australia	5	6	2	715	201	-	1	4	178.75	6
1948	England	England	5	9	2	508	173*	2	1	2	72.57	2
Total			**52**	**80**	**10**	**6996**	**334**	**7**	**13**	**29**	**99.94**	**32**

Opponents	M	Inn	NO	Runs	HS	0s	50	100	Avrge	Ct
ENGLAND	37	63	7	5028	334	6	12	19	89.79	20
INDIA	5	6	2	715	201	-	1	4	178.75	6
SOUTH AFRICA	5	5	1	806	299*	-	-	4	201.50	2
WEST INDIES	5	6	-	447	223	1	-	2	74.50	4

Venues in Australia	M	Inn	NO	Runs	HS	0s	50	100	Avrge	Ct
Adelaide	7	11	2	970	299*	1	3	3	107.78	6
Brisbane ('Gabba)	5	7	-	736	226	1	1	3	105.14	4
Brisbane (Exhibition Grnd)	2	3	-	242	223	-	-	1	80.67	2
Melbourne	11	17	4	1671	270	1	3	9	128.54	9
Sydney	8	12	-	703	234	2	3	2	58.58	6
Total	**33**	**50**	**6**	**4322**	**299***	**5**	**10**	**18**	**98.23**	**27**

Venues in England	M	Inn	NO	Runs	HS	0s	50	100	Avrge	Ct
Leeds	4	6	1	963	334	-	-	4	192.60	1
Lord's	4	8	1	551	254	-	1	2	78.71	1
Manchester	3	4	1	81	30*	-	-	-	27.00	2
Nottingham	4	8	1	526	144*	1	1	3	75.14	-
The Oval	4	4	-	553	244	1	1	2	138.25	1
Total	**19**	**30**	**4**	**2674**	**334**	**2**	**3**	**11**	**102.85**	**5**

100s	Opponent	Venue	Season
112	England	Melbourne	1928–29
123	England	Melbourne	1928–29
131	England	Nottingham	1930
254	England	Lord's	1930
334	England	Leeds	1930
232	England	The Oval	1930
223	West Indies	Brisbane	1930–31
152	West Indies	Melbourne	1930–31
226	South Africa	Brisbane	1931–32
112	South Africa	Sydney	1931–32
167	South Africa	Melbourne	1931–32
299*	South Africa	Adelaide	1931–32
103*	England	Melbourne	1932–33
304	England	Leeds	1934
244	England	The Oval	1934
270	England	Melbourne	1936–37
212	England	Adelaide	1936–37
169	England	Melbourne	1936–37
144*	England	Nottingham	1938
102*	England	Lord's	1938
103	England	Leeds	1938
187	England	Brisbane	1946–47
234	England	Sydney	1946–47
185	India	Brisbane	1947–48
132	India	Melbourne	1947–48
127*	India	Melbourne	1947–48
201	India	Adelaide	1947–48
138	England	Nottingham	1948
173*	England	Leeds	1948

First-Class Career
Debut: 1927–28 New South Wales v South Australia, Adelaide

	M	Inn	NO	Runs	HS	0s	50	100	Avrge	Ct
First-Class	234	338	43	28067	452*	6	69	117	95.14	131
Sheffield Shield	62	96	15	8926	452*	5	20	36	110.20	38
First-Class for NSW	41	69	10	5813	452*	3	17	21	98.53	17
First-Class for SA	44	63	8	5753	369	3	12	25	104.60	36

Highest Score: 452* New South Wales v Queensland, Sydney, 1929–30
Best Bowling: 3-35 Australian XI v Cambridge University, Cambridge, 1930